A gift of Dennis
TReaudeau

Feb 1991

Fly Tying and
Fishing for
Panfish and Bass

D1733716

Tom Keith

DEMCO

Frank Amato Publications
P.O. Box 82112 • Portland, Oregon 97282
(503) 653-8108

DEDICATION

To Susie

We'll always remember

_____

_____ ACKNOWLEDGEMENTS

A special thanks to the people who helped bring this book about. First to Linda, exceptional fly tyer and photographer who has put up a lot, both before and during this project, and the only person I know who is as enthusiastic about fishing as I am. Thanks to Rich Farley, a longtime friend who helped with processing photographs during the early going; Verl Borg for acting as model and consultant; and Jeff Blaser, fisheries biologist, who has taught me a good deal about fish, their needs and habits, and is never too busy to answer my questions.

Copyright 1989 — Tom Keith
Book Design: Joyce Herbst — Typesetting: John F. Michael
Illustrations: Esther Poleo — Printed in U.S.A.
ISBN: 0-936608-80-3

CONTENTS

INTRODUCTION

I remember the frustration I experienced the day I bought my first fly rod. I walked into the fishing department of a large sporting goods store and stood in front of an old wooden rack stuck back in a dark corner that held a couple of dozen fly rods. I recognized them as being fly rods because of their general shape, but aside from the obvious differences of length and color, I couldn't tell one from the other.

I didn't know the first thing about fly fishing except that I had enjoyed magazine stories by Ted Trueblood and Erwin Bauer that gave glowing accounts of trout fishing in the Rockies. That was enough for me – I had to learn to fly fish.

My problem was, I didn't know the first thing about fly fishing or what kind of gear to choose, I thought I could just walk into a store, buy a rod and reel, and start filling the freezer with fillets. Heck, I'd been catching all the catfish, bullheads, bluegill and crappie I could carry with bait cast and spinning gear since I was a kid, and I didn't think there was any reason this kind of fishing would be different.

Fly fishing wasn't – and isn't – Nebraska's most popular sport, and the clerk who helped me knew as much about it as I did. Together we examined each rod and I flexed each one against the floor like I would a spinning rod to determine its action. I narrowed the field to the ones I thought felt about right, and made my final decision by comparing price tags. After 20 minutes in the store, I walked out with a $20 fiberglass rod, $8 reel, $10 line and a couple of gaudy flies that cost about 15 cents each.

Once home, I put my new outfit together and went out into the backyard to learn to cast. It was a long, time-consuming battle, but I eventually got to the point where I could whip the line out about 15 feet if I used my whole body to power the rod. It never occurred to me that I would have done much better if I hadn't purchased a 9 foot long, 8-weight rod and a 6-weight level line to use with it. I have never been good at reading directions and the only numbers on the rod and line box I'd been concerned with were the prices.

I was in a hurry to try out my new equipment and figured it would be just as easy to practice casting at a small pond I had permission to fish. When I arrived it dawned on me that the large diameter green fly line just wasn't going to go through the eye of my size 10 flies. In my haste and inexperience, I'd forgotten to buy a leader and the clerk hadn't pointed out my error. Luckily I had a spinning rod in the car, so I clipped a length of 6-pound monofilament, about 18 inches long, from the reel and hoping it wouldn't be too long, tied it to the end of my fly line. I knotted on one of my flies, something yellow, green and pink, to the end of my leader and made my first cast.

Recounting the afternoon in detail would only embarrass me, so I'll just say that during the next few hours I gave new meaning to the term beating the water to a froth.

There were a few occasions when I was somehow able to make a crude near-cast, when the line actually went forward a short distance and the fly landed in the water. More often the fly was hung-up in bushes, weeds, trees and once even stuck on the only partially submerged stump in the whole pond. But, I was determined to learn, so I kept telling myself how much fun I was having, and I even managed to catch a small bluegill. I was having trouble with my equipment, but I was also having fun and when I accidentally caught that first fish with my fly gear I was hooked deeper than he was.

Suddenly Trueblood and Bauer weren't the only guys who could catch fish on a fly rod, they just had better places to fish. I spent a couple enjoyable hours trying to catch another fish, but the one I caught must have been the last in the pond because I didn't get another strike all afternoon. That evening I was back in my stack of magazines reading articles by Jason Lucas and Ray Bergman, gathering tips to improve my flyrodding knowledge and technique.

I started talking about fly fishing at work and one of the guys told me about all the fun he was having tying his own flies and how much money he was saving in the process. He gave me the address of a mail-order house called Herter's Inc., then located in Waseca, Minnesota. They sold all kinds of fishing, fly tying and other outdoor equipment. I sent for a catalog, and its arrival in my mailbox changed my life forever.

I quickly learned why I was having trouble with my equipment so I replaced it with the right combination of rod, reel, line, leader and fly. But, I didn't stop there. I really enjoyed fishing with my fly gear and as I was having some success catching bluegill now and then, all I wanted to do was fish more.

Then there was that inch-thick Herter's catalog filled with color pictures of all kinds of exotic fly tying materials from feathers and furs to tinsels and flosses. It happened just like Jerry Clower says it always does; that catalog flung a cravin' on me, and I started ordering fly tying tools and materials.

Since my first fly fishing experience 27 years ago, I've accumulated a shameful amount of fly fishing and fly tying equipment and materials, and I've been lucky enough to spend more time fishing than many people spend working. Recently I've even started to feel a little guilty about it, and I don't always admit to the amount of time I spend fishing. But, just between you and me . . .

Today I'm glad I learned about fly fishing the hard way because it gives me some insight into the problems other people have and has helped me immensely in teaching others to enjoy the sport.

My wife, Linda, is the only person I know who likes to fish as much as I do, and that's the ideal situation. She's also a darn good photographer and most of the photos in this book, as well as most of those that appear with my magazine articles, are hers.

Through the years we've been involved in a number of fishing-related activities. I've sold fishing equipment, owned a rod and reel repair shop, taught fishing classes, and presented a variety of programs to various groups. Linda and I taught fly tying classes for more than 10 years, and Linda owned and operated her own small fly tying business for several years. She recently gave up that business to devote all of her time to photography.

This book is largely opinion, but we don't apologize because the information is based on a lot of time and experience at the tying bench and on the water. We know the information is accurate and we can vouch for each technique. We want you to realize there are many ways to do the things we will discuss, some of those will not be as reliable or as effective as those we suggest, and some may be just as good or even better, but we're going to tell you what works well for us, and we're confident our techniques will work well for you.

Above all, the information in this book will be practical — you can read about it one minute and do it the next. You won't find much fluff here, no elegant prose or penetrating concepts, just information that will help you enjoy your leisure time more and have a good time catching panfish and bass with your fly fishing gear. We hope it will give you the basis and encouragement to begin or continue fly tying and fishing and that you'll read other books to expand your fishing knowledge and techniques. If, when you're done reading this book you can tie a fly, catch a fish, and have a good time doing both, we'll consider it a success.

We believe life's too short to wander through it without enjoying the beauty and bounty of our outdoor resources. Verl Borg, a fishing partner and all-around good guy who provided help with the concept of this book and modeled for some of the photos, loves fly fishing in general and happens to like trout fishing in particular, but not for the usual reasons. "I like trout fishing because I enjoy being in the places where trout live. I enjoy catching fish, but that's not WHY I fish. I fish for enjoyment, for the camaraderie, for the experience of being outdoors, for the opportunity to see all the things I get to see when I'm fishing. Fishing is a funny sport. It can be very exciting, or it can be as boring as the day is long if the only object is to catch fish. I'm never bored when I'm fishing."

We want to help people catch fish, both by tying appropriate patterns and by learning where, when and how to use them. But we also hope our readers will enjoy the total fishing experience and have the pleasure of appreciating their outdoor surroundings.

So why did we write a book about tying and fishing flies for panfish and bass? The main reason is because many people think the term "fly fishing" is synonymous with "trout fishing" and that's really too bad. Too often people have the notion that because they have little opportunity to fish for trout there is no reason for them to try fly fishing. Actually, fishing for and learning to consistently catch warm water species from standing waters can be just as exciting and difficult as consistently catching trout from cold-water streams.

I am not taking anything away from trout fishing. It is an engrossing and tremendously interesting sport, but it is not the only worthwhile pursuit for the fly fisherman. The fact is, not everyone is lucky enough to live within driving distance of a trout stream, and economic conditions being what they are, not many people can travel to trout fishing areas as often as they'd like. But that doesn't mean that anyone who wants to enjoy the sport of fly fishing can't participate because of geographical or economic considerations.

Fishing is meant to be an enjoyable recreational pursuit. I think catching fish on a fly rod is great sport, whether it's bluegill, crappie and bass — the species we are concerned with in this book — or other species like northern pike, tiger muskie, salmon or carp.

Many fishermen take their sport very seriously; they take a great deal of pride in their equipment and their ability to use it well. Some even show disdain for other fishermen who don't pursue the same species in the same manner as they do. Some participate only in competitive fishing and are more interested in winning the contest or tournament than enjoying the fishing experience. C'mon you guys, fishing is supposed to be fun!

We hope you'll give it a try.
Tom Keith
Lincoln, Nebraska
1987

PART I

FISHING EQUIPMENT

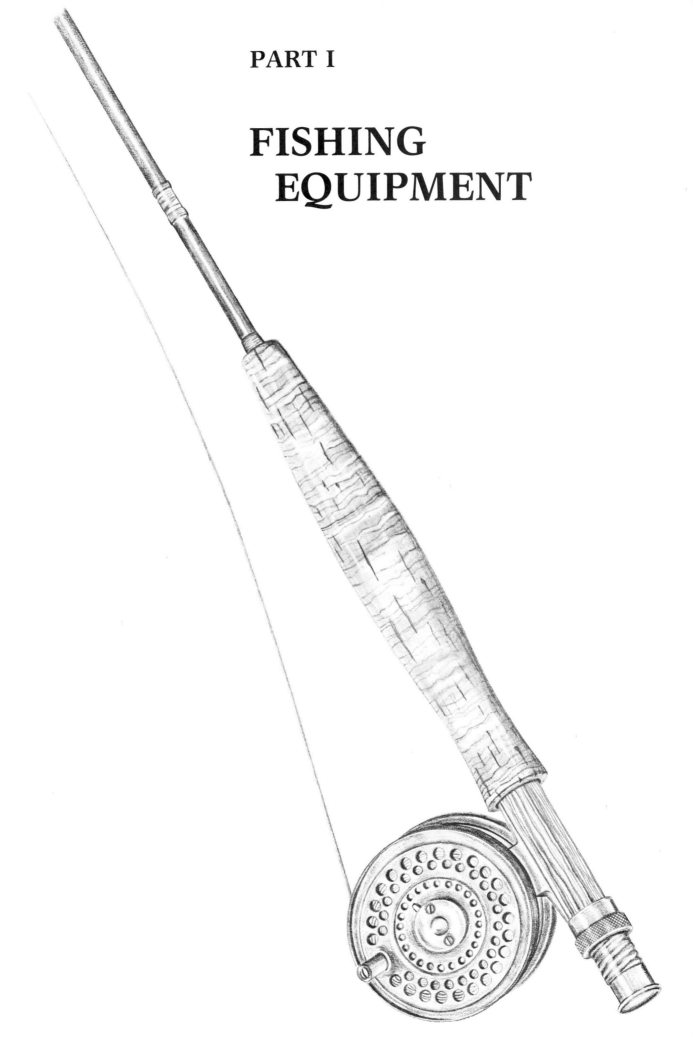

PUTTING YOUR OUTFIT TOGETHER

The hardest thing about getting started fly fishing is accumulating the right equipment. That can be a real chore if you are unfamiliar with what gear is available and don't have a basic idea about what you should choose for the kind of fishing you will be doing. Here are our recommendations for choosing affordable, practical fishing gear for panfish and bass.

RODS

There are as many types of fly rods as there are types of fishermen. If you are a beginning fly fisherman you are likely to be overwhelmed by the large number and variety of rods displayed before you the first time you walk into a fly fishing shop or the fly fishing department of a large sporting goods store. To help you choose one that is best suited for your needs, be sure you consider the following five things before leaving home to buy a rod.

1. Decide what kind of fishing you want to do with your rod. If you are interested in fishing only for panfish you should choose a shorter rod with lighter action than you would choose if you were planning to spend your time pursuing bass.

2. Decide what kind of water you will be fishing. Concentrating on large open water ponds and lakes offers you the opportunity to choose from a wider variety of rods than would be practical if you were planning on fishing small creeks or streams which typically have heavy aquatic vegetation and tall weed growth along the banks.

3. Decide what kind of lures and flies you will most often use because they will have a bearing on the type of fishing you'll be doing and the amount of backbone you'll need in your fly rod.

4. Have a price range in mind. There is some truth in the idea that more expensive, higher quality rods are more pleasing to use and generally perform better than cheaper rods. But, unless you have an unlimited budget, we recommend you begin with an inexpensive rod. A beginning fly fisherman is apt to treat his equipment a little rough while he's learning to cast and fish, and believe me, it is much easier to replace an inexpensive rod than a very expensive one if accidental damage occurs. It also makes sense to give yourself an opportunity to try fly fishing for a while to see if you like it before sinking a lot of money into equipment you may not use. Further, we believe it is beneficial to learn casting basics on equipment that is a little slower in its responses and more forgiving of initial mistakes. It's like learning to drive in an older, slower vehicle rather than in a souped-up high-tech sports car. Get your feet wet slowly, you can always move up to more expensive, faster responding gear as you go along.

5. There are rods available for all-around use, but if you choose one of them you should be aware that it won't perform as well as a rods specifically designed for the particular fishing you want to do. In other words, an 8 or 8½-foot long, 7-weight rod is considered to be a standard, medium-weight rod that will perform well for either panfish or bass fishing. If you want to use one rod exclusively for panfish, we recommend a 5-weight rod about 7 feet long; if you want to concentrate on bass fishing, a longer, heavier rod would be a better choice, something in the 9 to 9½-foot long class, and built to handle 9-weight lines. A rod of that design has plenty of backbone and can handle large bass under most conditions.

Panfish Rod

When you shop for a panfish rod we recommend you choose something in the neighborhood of a 7-foot long, 5-weight rod. This size rod is very easy to use, you can cast it all day without tiring yourself , and it won't overpower you. In other words, you'll have lots of fun catching panfish on this size rod.

Some experienced fly rodders prefer much longer rods, for instance, we have a friend who uses a 9-foot graphite rod rated for use with 4-weight line and has a ball catching panfish with it. The extra length allows him to cast further than he can with a shorter rod, but in most situations it's not much of an advantage, because rarely are casts in bluegill fishing more than 30 feet, a distance easily handled by most 7-foot rods. But, he made the rod himself and likes it a lot because of the way a chunky bluegill can bend it almost double. We recommend tackle we believe is best suited for the majority of fishermen to use in a variety of situations, but we also encourage fishermen to use whatever rod they enjoy using and can handle well.

Bass Rods

A heavier, stiffer rod is highly recommended for bass fishing – the same length and weight you'd choose for salmon fishing. You need a rod with enough backbone to handle an enraged 6- to 10-pound largemouth bent on throwing a hook and putting distance between the two of you. A good all-round choice for most bass fishing is an 8- to 9-foot fiberglass or graphite rod rated for the appropriate size line.

We prefer a medium, medium-slow or slow action rod because the slow action has the power to horse heavy bass from heavy cover, turn bulky bass bugs and poppers over during the cast and its full flexing ability is less tiring to use during a full day's fishing.

The material a rod contains is very important for many reasons. First is price: a fiberglass rod will be less expensive than a graphite rod of the same length, design, and recommended line weight. It is the ideal choice for a beginner because it is easily affordable and will take more punishment than a delicate graphite rod. If it is broken it can be easily repaired at home or in-expensively replaced.

Fiberglass rods weight more than graphite, but we don't think that is a handicap for a beginning caster. In fact, we think the extra weight makes a novice more aware of his casting motion and causes him to concentrate more on what he is doing. That helps him master the proper casting motion quicker than he would if using a lighter rod.

Graphite, on the other hand, is a more expensive material and is much lighter, more responsive and more sensitive. Its light weight allows even the most inexperienced angler to cast for long periods of time without becoming fatigued. It is more responsive, so there is no need to power or force a cast, and the rod's sensitivity lets the angler make delicate casts, feel exactly what is happening with his fly, and to detect even the softest strikes.

That description may give the impression that a graphite rod is a delicate tool, but it is actually a strong material that will withstand reasonable use for many years of fishing. No rod can take being slammed in a car door or trunk lid; if you step on the tip of any rod it will probably break. But, in all my years of operating a rod and reel repair business, I never saw a fly rod – either fiberglass or graphite – that had honestly snapped just from the stress of fighting a fish. That doesn't mean fishing stress NEVER breaks a rod, it just means that it rarely happens under normal conditions.

For many years fly rods were made only of bamboo and many bamboo rods are still being sold and used today. They are used mostly by anglers who enjoy the traditional aspects of fishing with a bamboo rod; some fishermen say they enjoy the feel of casting a slower rod; and others use a particular bamboo rod that was handed down from their grandfather and therefore they feel a special attachment to it.

But, a bamboo rod is not a practical tool for a novice angler. In the first place, quality bamboo rods are very expensive and that cost usually makes them prohibitive to the casual angler. The bamboo rod's action is extremely slow and is very difficult for most inexperienced fly rodders to use. But, there is no denying there is something very appealing about an old bamboo rod. Occasionally you pick one up at an antique or second-hand store for a reasonable price. Second-hand rods usually need some work, but refinishing, rewrapping and reconstructing a rod makes an interesting and relaxing winter project. And, the rod sure looks nice over the mantel or in the rod rack when you're finished with it.

The rod's action is the amount it flexes during a cast and the manner in which the flex is accomplished. A slow-action rod starts to bend closer to the rod butt than faster actions do, and the rod tip moves slowly. This type of action is very powerful and ideal for casting heavy, bulky bass bugs, flies and poppers. By contrast, a medium-action rod bends closer to the rod tip and the tip moves faster during the cast. It is a good choice for casting normal-size streamers, wet flies, nymphs, and some larger dry flies. A fast-action rod flexes only near the rod tip and causes the tip to move rapidly during the cast. It is the choice of many dry fly fishermen.

When you choose your rod be sure it has an ample number of line guides to keep the line close to the rod and eliminate the tendency of the line to hit the rod during the cast. The line should shoot through the guides easily and unhampered and should feel smooth and fluid when cast. The first guide, known as the stripper guide, should be located at least 20 inches from the front portion of the rod grip to ensure good casting performance. Examine all windings on the rod to be sure they are tight and well lacquered.

Be sure to examine the ferrules carefully. If you are buying a fiberglass rod it will have either metal ferrules or the more popular internal fiberglass-to-fiberglass ferrules. Metal ferrules are less attractive than internal ferrules that look as though there is no joint at all, but they have the advantage of being easily replaced if they become worn. If the internal ferrule becomes worn, you usually have two choices — to live with the loose joint or replace the rod. Whichever type you choose, be sure the ferrules fit together tightly and that the tip portion of the rod doesn't slip and turn as you cast.

Be sure your reel fits well on the reel seat, that the fittings close sufficiently to grip the reel feet tightly, and that the reel seat is immovable on the rod blank.

The grip should feel comfortable in your hand and you should like the overall appearance of the rod. Get one you like the looks of and is easy to handle because you'll have to get along with it for a long time.

REELS

There are basically only two types of fly reels, *single-action* and *automatic*. Single-action reels are operated by manually turning the spool with your hand, much like any other kind of fishing reel you may be accustomed to using. An automatic reel has a large internal spring that winds as line is stripped from the reel, then retrieves the line rapidly when the angler presses a lever or trigger mechanism releasing the spring. Most bass and panfish anglers choose single-action models both for ease of operation and dependability. A single-action reel operates exactly as the name implies, one

turn of the handle makes the spool rotate once, retrieving a relatively small amount of line with each turn. Multiplier reels look like common single-action reels, but they are designed so that each turn of the handle turns the spools more than once and retrieves a larger amount of line each time it turns.

Most quality single-action and multiplier reels allow fishermen to switch spools easily and rapidly. In addition to being very handy, this saves the angler money because there is no need for him to purchase a separate reel for each line to be used with a particular rod. One reel and several additional spools will serve the same purpose as several reels with one spool each.

Automatic reels may be useful in some situations, but they severely limit the angler in many ways. There is little room for backing on most automatic reels, they do not have adjustable drag systems, and there is no possibility of quickly changing the spool to use a different type of line. Automatic reels are generally quite heavy and have little to offer panfish and bass fishermen.

Reels are available in a variety of weights, sizes and capacities. They are rated for use with specific line weights and are designed to compliment the rod being used. For instance, a reel made to be used with a 4, 5, or 6-weight line and a short, light rod is smaller and lighter than one designed to hold 7, 8, or 9-weight line and to be used with a correspondingly longer, heavier rod.

You should choose a panfishing reel that is light weight and has the capacity to hold 30 to 50 yards of backing along with the fly line and leader. Seldom, if ever, will a panfish be large enough or strong enough to take all of the fly line from the reel making it necessary for you to use the backing while playing the fish. But, the backing has another purpose, it increases the spool's arbor size to prevent tiny, tight loops from forming in the part of the fly line that is wrapped near the spool.

On the other hand, bass fishermen may occasionally hook a fish in the 3 to 9-pound class and have to give up the full line and a fair amount of backing to avoid loosing the fish to a broken leader. Because of that potential many bass fishermen choose large capacity reels and wind 75 to 100 yards of backing behind their fly lines so they'll have the longer length available if they hook a large fish.

Do you buy a right-hand or left-handed model reel? We recommend right-handed anglers use a reel that winds from the left side, which eliminates the need to cast with one hand then switch the rod to the other hand to reel or fight a fish. Of course, south paws should choose reels that wind from the right hand. Fortunately finding a right or left hand reel is not a problem, because nearly all of today's single action fly reels can be easily converted from left-hand to right-hand retrieves and vice-versa. Just follow the instruction sheet included with each reel.

The drag system is another feature to consider when choosing your reel. One of the primary functions of the drag is to keep the line from free-spooling and over-running as it is pulled from the reel. For panfishing a simple click-pawl system works well, but if you are going after heavy-weight bass, consider buying a reel with an exposed spool flange that allows you to slow the turning spool by pressing the palm of your hand against it, a technique called "palming the reel." All you have to do to check a reel's click-pawl drag is hold the reel securely in one hand and jerk an amount of line from the spool. If the line pulls off the spool too easily or overruns the spool, tighten the drag and try it again. If it happens a second time, choose another reel.

Some of the better and more expensive reels have spools that are mounted on ball bearings and are self-lubricating, and others are counterbalanced to eliminate spool wobble when a large fish strips line from the reel.

Today's reels are generally made of light weight, durable metals with high luster finishes. Aluminum reels are light and dependable, and graphite reels are even lighter, but predictably more expensive. There is a great deal of difference in the performance of a $10 reel and that of a $200 reel, but as far as actual functional necessity and practicality, the less expensive models, say in the $40 to $70 class will perform well for the average angler through many years of panfish and bass fishing.

In our opinion a fisherman on a limited budget is better off spending a little more for his rod and cutting back on the cost of his reel. Originally, all the fly reel was expected to do was hold the line, and though modern technology has greatly improved its design and function, a bass or panfish angler can still get by nicely using the reel as it was first intended. In panfish and bass fly fishing the fly reel is not as important a tool as a spinning reel or bait casting reel — they both require that the reel be an integral component of every cast and virtually every fish hooked is played directly from the reel — this is not always necessary with a fly reel.

LINES

To the average fly fisherman the most confusing part of building a usable fishing system is choosing the proper fly line for the type of fishing he wants to do. But, that need not be the case — there really isn't much you have to learn to understand what fly lines are all about.

A fly line is constructed with a core of braided nylon and an extremely flexible plastic or vinyl covering. That covering is what determines the line's shape and provides a uniformly smooth surface that passes easily through the rod guides.

Fly lines have many characteristics: *taper, weight, behavior,* and *color.* Each of these characteristics is clearly marked on the line's packaging and must be considered before you make a purchase.

"Taper" refers to the shape of the line. There are four basic tapers and each is designed to do a specific job:

L — Level Line

A level line actually is level, or the same diameter throughout its entire length. It is generally the least expensive line on the shelf, but it is a poor choice for panfish and bass fishing in most situations. Level lines tend to be cumbersome and difficult for a novice fisherman to cast. Its design makes it adequate for short casts but its effective range, even in the hands of most experienced anglers, is in the area of 30 feet. It is difficult to control at greater distances and is too bulky to roll cast well.

DT — Double Taper

This line is tapered at each end and has a constant diameter throughout the middle section. The tapered forward section lets the fisherman make accurate casts at reasonable distances and because the line weighs less in the tip, it presents a fly very delicately, a real advantage when the fish are spooky. The double tapered line is also easy on the billfold because when one end begins to show signs of wear the line can be reversed to double its life.

WF — Weight Forward

A weight forward line is the best choice for a fly fisherman who is learning to cast. It has a heavy section near the front end and a long narrow mid-section that helps to shoot the line to accomplish longer casts. A weight forward line performs well at all casting distances and is the ideal choice for virtually all bass and panfish fishing. The extra weight at the front of the line helps torque the rod and makes casting in windy situations less of a chore. The "bass bug taper" has an even more radical taper at the front of the standard weight forward line and makes casting heavy wind-resistant bass bugs less difficult. Serious bass fishermen should own a bass bug taper line or two.

SH — Shooting Head

A shooting head is a 30-foot length of double-taper or level line secured to a length of very small diameter level line or strong monofilament that allows the fisherman to make very long casts, sometimes 100 feet or more. It can be an effective tool in the hands of an experienced fishermen, but has little or no application for panfish or bass fishing.

The line's weight is expressed as a numerical designation determined by weighing the first 30 feet of the line, excluding the line's tapered tip. The designation is a code developed by the American Fishing Tackle Manufacturer's Association (AFTMA) to maintain consistency throughout the market — for instance, all 7-weight lines weigh approximately the same regardless of brand name or manufacturer. There are 11 line weights available today, 2 through 12; 2 being the lightest, 12 the heaviest. The most popular, in terms of sales, are 6, 7 and 8 weights because they are middle-of-the-road sizes that can be used in a variety of situations.

Line Types

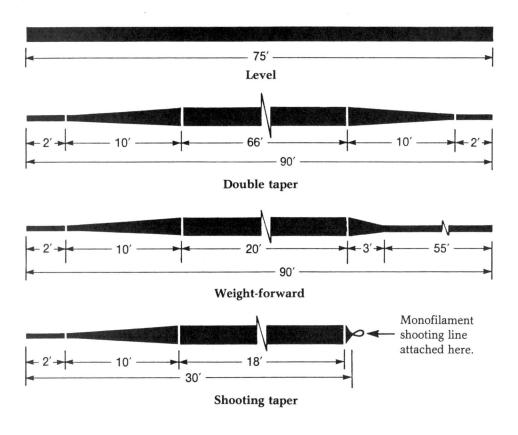

Buy a line that matches the weight of your rod. The line weight the rod was designed to handle, is printed on the rod blank near the grip. Trust that information and buy a line that matches your rod.

Some fishermen say they use a line one size heavier than recommended for their rod because the slightly heavier line helps to create more bend in the rod and makes it seem easier to cast, especially when throwing heavy, wind resistant bass bugs. We recommend you learn to use the correct combination effectively because you will develop a better casting technique by using a balanced outfit.

Looking for bluegill? Never pass up a spot where tree limbs have fallen into the water.

Lines used in panfish and bass fishing are also designated by function: *floating, floating/sinking,* and *sinking.*

The floating line is identified by the letter "F." As the name implies, it floats throughout its entire length and is used with all types of flies in shallow water or at shallow depths. Using a floating line does not mean a sinking fly won't sink, it means the fly will sink only as deep as the leader allows. Every panfish and bass fisherman must own at least one floating line to use the techniques discussed in this book.

The floating/sinking line, identified as "F/S," is a floating line that has a 10 to 15 foot long tip section that sinks. The sinking tip takes the fly deeper in the water, up to as much as 12 to 15 feet deep, while providing adequate line control. Because the longest portion of the line floats, it makes lifting line from the water at the beginning of the cast fairly easy, as opposed to the difficulties presented by casting a sinking line. An angler who fishes only for panfish will find he can get along with only a floating line if he chooses, though a floating/sinking line will increase his capabilities a great deal. On the other hand, someone who is interested in fishing for bass in various situations, will find a floating/sinking line to be a definite advantage in many situations. A floating/sinking line is a neutral color throughout its floating section, and the sinking tip is usually a darker color.

A sinking line is identified by the letter "S" and is used to sink a fly in fairly deep water, even as much as 25 feet or more, and keep it there. It is difficult to control a sinking line in the first portion of a cast because the line must be brought up through the water on the back-cast, but once it clears the water it casts well. Sinking lines have little use in panfishing, and limited application in most bass fishing situations. If you have an unlimited budget you should probably own a sinking line or two, but as a practical matter, you can get along well without one for using the techniques discussed in this book.

BACKING

When you buy a fly line be sure you also purchase a spool of backing. One hundred yards of 18-to 20-pound test dacron will work best. Backing is tied to the rear end of the fly line and is wound directly onto the reel spool ahead of the line. The line should wind to within 1/4 to 3/8 inch of the spool's rim and backing wound under the line makes this possible. The backing is wound around the spool shaft and increases the size of the shaft so the line is wound on the spool in larger, looser coils that eliminate tight coils and kinks in the line. It also allows more of the line to be retrieved with each turn of the reel handle. If you hook a large bass you may have to give him a lot of line, and some of the backing to avoid loosing him before he's landed. Usually you'll put about 50 yards of backing on your reel, but the exact amount should be determined only by how close the fly line winds to the edge of the spool rim. If you aren't sure how much backing you need on your particular reel with your line, wind the line on first, followed by the backing to determine how much the reel will hold, then reverse it and tie the backing to the reel spool shaft. Then wind it and the line back on. Backing is kind of like an insurance policy, you may never need it, but if you do, you'll be glad you have it.

LEADERS

There are two basic types of leaders, knotless and compound. We recommend knotless, tapered leaders for beginning fly fishermen. They are easier to use because you needn't tie them yourself, they are available in a variety of lengths and tapers, and they don't have knots up and down their length to collect moss and algae on every cast. They are relatively inexpensive and are available at virtually all tackle shops that handle fly fishing equipment.

Compound leaders are sections of monofilament tied together in various lengths of decreasing diameter and strength, making the leader taper from the heavy butt section to the delicate tippet. They can also be purchased pre-tied at most tackle shops. Many fishermen prefer to design and tie their own leaders for special fishing situations; as well as every day use, and have good success using them.

One advantage of the compound leader is that the tippet material can be easily replaced. Each time the angler removes a bit of material from a knotless tapered leader, the diameter of the new tip is a little larger than it was before. It isn't long before the fine tippet portion of the leader has been snipped away and what's left is fairly large diameter monofilament. To avoid this problem some fishermen choose to use a tapered leader as a base, and replace the tippet now and then with their own leader material, creating, in essence, a convenient combination of knotless and compound styles.

The four parts of a leader are: *the butt,* or heaviest part that attaches directly to the fly line; *the midsection,* a long tapered section which accounts for most of the leader's length; *the tip,* a short section that connects the midsection to the tippet; and *the tippet* itself, which is the smallest diameter material that determines the strength of the leader. The fly is tied to the tippet.

For most panfishing we prefer to use a 7½-foot tapered knotless leader from size 6x to 4x, or about 1½-pound tippet test to about 3-pound tippet test. For bass fishing we use 2x to 0x leaders, or about 3½-pound test to 8-pound test.

In reading leader specifications, the x refers to the leader's diameter. The larger the x number, the smaller the diameter. As a rule of thumb, you can determine what leader size to use by dividing the hook size by three. For instance, if you are using a size 12 fly, a 4x tippet would be about right.

Most knotless tapered leaders come in four sizes, 6-, 7½-, 9- and 12-foot. Generally, longer leaders are used with floating lines, while shorter leaders are used with sink tip or sinking lines, especially in very deep water, because they are easier to control and keep the fly near the bottom. An important point to remember is that the sinking line is heavier than the leader and the leader will try to float and curve upwards in the water, so a very short leader, say 18 to 24 inches long, will keep the fly deeper than a 7½-foot leader used on the same line, unless the fisherman is using a weighted fly in addition to the sinking line. But the 7½-foot leader is considered to be average length and may be used effectively under nearly all conditions for panfish and bass fishing. We believe a longer leader is a little more difficult for a beginning fly fisherman to control while he's learning to cast.

Our recommendations for a beginning panfish and bass fishing outfit are:

- a 7½-foot medium-action fiberglass rod rated for 7- or 8-weight line
- a weight-forward floating fly line matched to the weight of the rod
- an inexpensive single-action fly reel with the capacity to hold the fly line and at least 50 yards of backing
- three or four 7½-foot long knotless tapered leaders in appropriate tippet sizes. (Start with 4x for panfish and 2x for bass fishing)

Our recommendations for an angler of more experience who wants to specialize in panfishing:

- a 7-foot, 5-weight medium-action fiberglass or graphite rod
- a single-action fly reel of the appropriate size and weight to complement the short, light rod
- a weight-forward floating 5-weight fly line (a double taper line, a floating/sinking line are also useful on occasion, though not necessary) and the proper amount of backing
- a selection of knotless tapered leaders with tippet sizes from 3x to 6x

Our recommendations for an angler of more experience who wants to specialize in bass fishing:

- an 8-foot to 9½-foot fiberglass or graphite medium-slow or slow-action rod
- a weight forward line and a bass bug taper line, both rated to match the rod (a floating/sinking line will also be useful in some situations)
- a single-action reel with the capacity to hold the above lines and at least 50 yards of backing
- a selection of 7½-foot-long knotless tapered leaders with tippets ranging from 3x to 0x

MISCELLANEOUS EQUIPMENT

There are several miscellaneous items of gear a panfish or bass fly rodder should consider owning that will make his life on the water simpler and more enjoyable.

FISHING VEST

The fly fishing vest is an important piece of equipment and many anglers would rather give up their pants than be deprived of their fishing vest. Some vests are constructed as a combination fishing vest/life jacket and are an ideal accessory for people who don't swim well or are concerned about wading. A fly fishing vest is cut somewhat like a dress vest, but it has the capacity to store lots of fishing gear and other necessary items. A good fly vest is made from durable material and has strong, double-stitched seams. Its short length helps keep it from dragging in the water and some models have plastic-lined pockets so if the bottom of the vest does get wet, the items inside remain dry. A vest should fit well across the back and shoulders when zipped up the front. It should be loose enough to allow freedom for casting, but snug enough so it doesn't flop around during the casting motions.

A good vest has plenty of pockets for carrying all kinds of equipment, and that only makes sense, since it is the fly fisherman's tackle box. In the pockets of my vest I carry an assortment of fly boxes and hundreds of flies in every conceivable pattern, style and type. I carry spare leaders, a small first aid kit, dry fly floatant, a pair of small scissors, some metal strips for adding weight to the leader, insect repellent, a box of small poppers, a small scale/tape measure, waterproof matches, an emergency stringer, a tiny flashlight, a small wader patching kit, and a folded-up copy of our state's fishing regulations.

In the large rear pouch (I call it that because it looks similar to the game pouch on my hunting coat), I carry extra spools with various types of line for my reel, an extra reel, pipe, pipe tobacco, pipe cleaners, a butane lighter, a small candle for starting fires, usually a package or two of beef or venison jerky, often a can of Diet Coke, and sometimes a small camera and an extra roll or two of film.

Connected to "D" rings on the outside of the vest I have a fingernail clipper on a length of cord (a tool I use constantly while fishing), a pair of hemostats connected with another length of cord, and my trout-sized landing net.

There is a sheepskin patch sewn to one pocket where I stick water-soaked flies while they dry. I could get by with less gear, but I hate to look for something while I'm fishing and suddenly remember I left it in the car or on the tying bench. I believe in going prepared.

Fly vests come in a number of styles and sizes and our only advise is to get one that fits and has more pockets than you think you'll need. They fill up very quickly and you'll appreciate the extra space afforded by additional pockets.

FISHING HAT

Every fisherman needs a hat to shield his head and neck from the sun and occasionally, a bit of rain. I prefer hats with large brims because my eyes are a little sensitive to light, and large brims help me avoid headaches. Cowboy hats are my preference and I wear them a lot, except in the wind because I don't like to waste fishing time chasing my hat. When it's windy, I usually wear a baseball type cap. It does a fine job of shading my eyes, but it leaves my neck exposed so I have to keep an eye out for sunburn.

A fishing hat is the traditional place to store flies, and that's fine if you spend a couple of bucks and buy a sheepskin hat band to hook them in. Otherwise you'll end up cutting the flies out of the hat itself, because it's nearly impossible to remove a barbed hook from the close-knit materials that are used in most hats.

SUNGLASSES

Fishermen, like everyone else involved in any type of outdoor activity, should wear eye protection. You must protect your eyes, even if it is with your regular day-to-day spectacles, and to avoid eye strain, headaches and even sunburn, a fisherman should wear polarized sunglasses. These not only protect the eyes, they also eliminate glare and allow you to see below the surface of the water, a real advantage when looking for spawning areas, submerged weedbeds, and various kinds of cover. We always wear polarized glasses everywhere we fish.

Well equipped fly fisherman

FLOATING FISH BASKETS

If you are going to keep the fish you catch, they must be kept alive and healthy until they are cleaned. There is absolutely no better tool a still water fly fisherman can use for that purpose than a floating fish basket. The fish basket has a hinged door on the top that you open by pushing down with your hand. There is another hinged door on the bottom that allows easy removal of fish by pushing the door up. A plastic section in the top of the basket keeps it afloat. The basket is made of wire mesh and constructed to allow plenty of room for fish to be kept underwater in the basket without injuring them.

We tie the baskets to our float tubes or waders with cord, and they float along beside us handy and ready for instant use.

Stringers, on the other hand, whether rope or metal, are very hard on fish. Rope stringers are often threaded through the fish's mouth and out his gills, which holds him securely, but injures his gills and sometimes kills him. Sometimes large fish fight the stringer and ultimately tear their flesh enough that they get off and escape, only to later die of their injuries. Metal stringers are somewhat better in that most models have safety pin clips that hold the fish. One end of the clip is forced through the flesh in the fish's lower jaw, then snapped closed so it can't escape. This holds the fish, but holds it vertically in the water making it difficult for the fish to use its gills and it may die.

I also like fish baskets because they float, whether attached to the fisherman or not. Before I started using them, there were a few times when I lost stringers of fish because I hadn't tied the stringer properly to the tube or my waders, and it came loose and sank out of sight. Loosing a day's catch is not only discouraging, it's also a sad waste of fish.

Floating fish baskets can be purchased for around $10 in most tackle stores.

CLIPPERS

Of all my fishing tools, one of the most useful is a pair of fingernail clippers. It is ideal for cutting leaders, trimming up flies at the lake, and all the hundreds of other small cutting jobs that need to be done. We buy them by the dozen and scatter them throughout our equipment so there's always one handy.

HEMOSTATS

Hemostats are surgical forceps that are ideal for removing hooks from a fish's jaw or throat, and to hold very small flies while they are being tied on or modified in some way to match the fishing situation. Because the hemostat's jaws lock shut at the handle, many fishermen just clip them to their fly vests. I do that, but I also attach mine with a cord so I don't drop it in the water and loose it.

Hemostats are available from most fly and tackle shops and fishing equipment mail order houses.

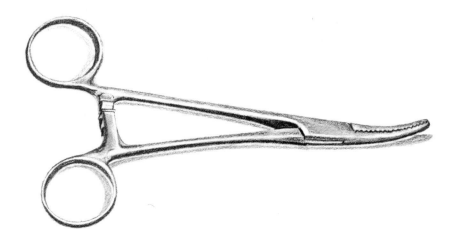

FLY BOXES

Fly boxes are made to hold flies. They are very necessary and important pieces of equipment, but we don't get over-excited about them. They are available in a variety of styles and a wide range of prices, but we recommend using less expensive, less fancy models for holding bass and panfish flies.

We like the plastic boxes with ripple foam inserts for holding most of our small streamers, nymphs, wet flies, and dry flies. We carry some of our dry flies in pill bottles purchased at the pharmacy, or in the round plastic containers that protect film canisters. Our small bass bugs go in larger plastic boxes and there is an entire multi-drawer tackle box reserved for the larger deerhair bass bugs, so the deerhair is not matted down during storage. Be sure to let your flies air-dry before storing them in boxes, both to preserve the materials, and to eliminate hook rusting.

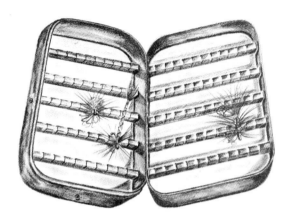

Fly Box

WADERS

Fly fishermen must be able to get into the water to effectively fish panfish and bass cover, and wading is most comfortable in a pair of good waders.

Obviously, if you are fishing from a boat or from shore, you can get by without waders, but those two tactics severely limit the areas you can fish and the techniques you can use.

We sometimes see barefoot fishermen wading along a lake's shoreline. Don't wade barefoot! You'd be amazed and appalled at the things people throw in the water — everything from empty beverage cans to broken bottles; old fish hooks to broken knives; all types of food containers to miscellaneous junk that has accumulated in the car trunk or the boat. There are also natural underwater hazards that can be tough on your feet, like the sharp ends of broken-off reeds, sharp rocks, tree limbs, branches and roots.

There are two basic types of waders on the market today. The old boot-foot wader comes in both insulated and regular models. These are heavy waders we use for cold weather duck and goose hunting, and they serve us well for fly fishing, too, especially in cool water. They are tough to protect your legs and bulky so you can wear warm clothes in them, if you wish. In the summer you must be sure to wear jeans or some type of long-legged garment inside your rubber waders. It will get warm and you'll probably do some sweating while wearing them, but if you go barelegged in this type of wader, the rubber will chafe the skin on your legs.

The new stocking-foot waders are made of softer, lighter, more flexible materials, aren't as baggy, and are more comfortable than most boot-foot models. You must wear a shoe with these, either a commercial wading shoe or, we've found old tennis or running shoes also work well. Stocking-foot waders are very functional, though you should think twice before charging through heavy cover which would not be an obstacle in more durable rubber boot-foot waders.

You will have to choose between hip waders and chest waders, and we strongly recommend chest waders for lake and pond fishing.

A good selection of float tubing gear for the fly fisherman. Swim fins are shown on the left tube, foot paddles are on the right tube. In the foreground on the right is a pair of ultra-light waders we use when float tubing.

You'll need a pair of durable suspenders that are not usually included when you buy waders. Choose suspenders with the widest straps you can find because narrow straps tend to dig into your shoulders and become uncomfortable in a short period of time. We also recommend wearing a belt around the outside of your waders. The belt will help keep water out and air in, so you can float with your feet up if you do stumble in deep water. Any old belt will do if it is large enough to fit comfortabley around the waders.

If you are buying waders to use with a float tube, you should choose the highest chest waders you can find, because when you sit on the tube's seat, the bending of your legs and knees automatically pulls the waders down. Linda and I have waders made especially for float tube use that are not only higher than normal models, they also have an inflatable section around the top that we blow up and then adjust to a tight, comfortable fit with a draw string. Because a tuber is sitting so close to the water's surface, he gets splashed occasionally and this inflatable feature keeps water from sloshing or dripping inside the waders. Our float tube waders are also very light weight, which is necessary to allow easy movement while propelling the tube.

When you are stream fishing, it is important to have a felt sole, corkers, or some type of metal studs or cleats affixed to the bottom of your waders to provide traction on slick rocks. In pond and lake wading regular soles are sufficient, but you should be aware of some other potential dangers. Wading fishermen sometimes trip or fall over submerged roots, branches or rocks; they step into deep holes, creek channels or muskrat runs; or they suddenly find themselves bogged in very soft, gripping mud on the lake bottom. Be aware of these problems and be very careful while wading, in fact, it is a good idea to wear a life preserver when wading unfamiliar waters.

FLOAT TUBES

Next to waders, float tubes (sometimes called belly boats) are the greatest advancement in panfish and bass fly fishing of recent years. Float tubes are inexpensive (well within the budget of most fishermen) and they give an angler the ability to fish waters that were inaccessible to him before. They let him approach the fish quietly, are easily transported, safe, comfortable, and easy to use.

There are many brands and styles of float tubes on the market, and though they all look similar, there are some important differences. We recommend you buy the best quality float tube you can afford.

Float tubes are basically large inflatable truck tire tubes fitted with a nylon cover. The angler sits in the hole in the middle of the tube on a seat supported by nylon straps. His legs dangle below and he moves his legs and feet to propel himself through the water. There are usually pockets for carrying gear sewn onto the nylon cover and an inflatable backrest to protect the angler from waves sloshing over the back of the tube and drenching him from behind.

When you are shopping for a tube, choose one that has good workmanship. The cover's seams should be well sewn with double and triple stitching. The nylon zippers on the equipment pockets should work without binding and have large tabs that are easy to locate and grab. The mesh seat's safety release should work easily, so the tube can be shed quickly in an emergency. The backrest should be high enough to protect the angler from water splashing from behind and the tube large enough overall to support the size and weight of the individual fisherman (they come in different sizes).

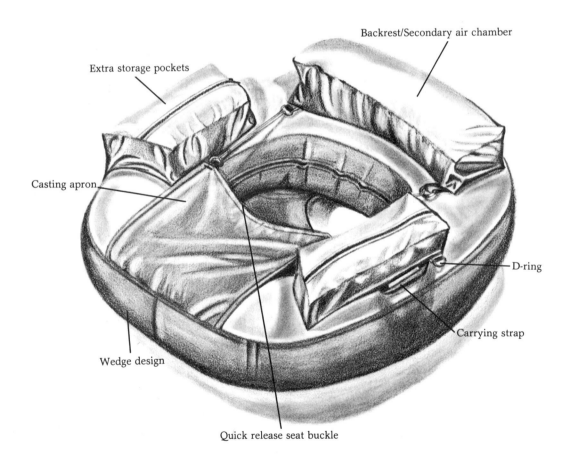

Backrest/Secondary air chamber

Extra storage pockets

Casting apron

D-ring

Carrying strap

Wedge design

Quick release seat buckle

Those things are basic requirements for buying any float tube, and there are a few extras we suggest you consider before buying a tube that will be used extensively for fly fishing.

Choose a tube that has plenty of pockets. Some inexpensive tubes have only one pocket and you may be able to get by with it for a while, but we've found we never have enough pockets, so we recommend buying a model that has at least two, and preferably three large pockets. A fly fisherman will need the apron feature that keeps his fly line at tube level so it does not fall down around his legs and become tangled. The apron is a piece of nylon material that is sewn to the front of the nylon covering and attaches to the covering behind the angler by means of two elastic cords with plastic fasteners. The cords are easy to hook and the apron fits snugly around the angler's lower chest.

Also choose a model that has several 'D' rings sewn at various locations on the outside of the nylon cover. The rings are handy for attaching things, like bungy cords for securing another rod to the tube; a rope securing a floating fish basket; a line securing an extra life jacket; or just to hook over the head of a large nail on the garage wall to hang the tube.

The tube and the nylon covering are pretty tough, but just to be on the safe side, carry a tube patching kit with you to stop unexpected leaks and a bicycle-style hand pump for adding air in an emergency. Though we've had our tubes for several years and have used them hard, we have never had a puncture or other type of tube problem.

The fisherman propels his tube by moving his feet and legs. You can purchase large heavy duty tube fins that resemble swim fins and move the tube when you slowly kick your legs. The fins propel you backwards through the water.

Fins work well, but we like to use plastic flippers much more. They attach around your ankles with a strap and have a molded heelseat for your heel and hinged flippers that extend from the outside edge of your ankle. When you lift your leg forward in the water, the hinged flipper folds back against your ankle. When you pull your leg down, the flipper moves forward and stops perpendicular to your ankle, so as you pull your leg back, the thrust moves you ahead. The advantage is that the movement is much like walking straight-legged and, most important, you move forward through the water rather than traveling backwards. We like to be able to see how close we are getting to the spots we want to fish, which we can't do if we're using fins and moving backwards. We think the movement necessary to propel the tube with flippers is easier and less tiring than using fins.

Some float tubes have extra-high backrests with a brilliant red or hunter orange covering that can be easily seen by boaters. We have also seen tubers on the lake with red or hunter orange flags flying from long plastic poles above their tubes, like kids use to decorate their bicycles and supermarket managers put on their grocery carts so they can find them easily in the parking lot.

The only drawback to a float tube is that it is hard to operate in the wind or against good-sized waves, but in the long run that is probably an advantage, because it makes tubers get off the lake when the weather is getting rough. Float tubes are intended to be used near shore, not in the middle of large lakes as substitute for a boat.

BOATS

Fly fishing from a boat is an excellent method for fishing hard to reach places surrounded by deep water or heavy vegetation, but it can also present some problems.

Canoes are a good choice for fly fishing because they are quiet, slow moving, and can be used in fairly shallow water. But, there is a correct method of fishing from a canoe. If you are alone, sit in the rear and make your casts forward on either side of the canoe. This gives you better control of the canoe and allows you to see where you are going while you cast, which makes steering much easier. If there are two people in the canoe, the fisherman should sit in the front and cast to likely looking water while the person in back guides and paddles the canoe. This allows the person in front to concentrate on his fishing without being preoccupied with the possibility of tangling his line with the person behind him. The person in front should fish for a time, then trade places with the person in back and let him fish for a while. In this manner, you will avoid the confusion of two people fly casting from the same canoe at the same time.

Small boats, like canoes, can serve as transportation and a fishing platform for fly fishermen, but they can also be frustrating to use. People tend to put too much gear and stuff in a boat, and a fly line, when being retrieved, can find millions of new and interesting ways of getting tangled in, under, around and through all that gear. Many boats also have lots of corners, gauges, dials, knobs, switches, graphs, and other objects that can snag a fly line. The one-at-a-time fly fishing rule applies to small boats too, both for convenience and safety. Many people are surprised at how difficult it is to cast a fly line while sitting in a boat the first few times they try it. It is different, but the technique can be mastered with a little practice.

There are two types of boats we feel are ideal for fly fishing. One is the modern bass boat that is low, wide and very stable in the water. Most bass boats have large flat deck areas that let fly fishermen stand while casting and provide a flat carpeted floor where the line can fall when being retrieved. Just remember to keep gear out of the way to avoid line tangles.

Our second choice for an ideal fly fishing boat is a pontoon boat. It has a large, flat deck that lets the fisherman move around a good-sized space while casting. It is comfortable for fishing just by virtue of its size and can be maneuvered surprisingly well in small spaces and in shallow water.

Whatever type of boat is used, it must be operated slowly, carefully and quietly during fishing. Never move the boat closer to the area you are fishing than necessary or you'll scare the fish. The person operating the boat should move it slowly, so the fisherman can cover each area thoroughly, and he must be constantly aware of where the boat is going to avoid hitting obstructions in the water or passing through good fishing spots.

_____ CATCH AND RELEASE

There was a time, not long ago, when people fished primarily to put food on the table. Releasing a fish after catching it was an uncommon practice, and having a successful day usually meant heading home with a full limit or a heavy stringer of fish.

Conditions were different then, there wasn't nearly the fishing pressure we see today, because few people fished regularly. But today people have more free time, more money to spend on hobbies and leisure time activities, and are much more mobile than they were even a decade ago.

It used to be that most people who fished used live baits, either worms or minnows, inexpensive equipment and they fished from shore. As a rule most any fish landed was headed for the frying pan, with the only exception being those that were just too small to clean.

More often than not, if the under-sized fish was a bluegill or crappie, it was tossed onto the bank rather than returned to the water because people thought so many small fish in a body of water caused stunting and the pond or lake would be ruined if too many small fish were present. Another reason many small fish were not returned to the water is a good number of them swallowed the bait and were severely injured as the hook was being removed. Small bleeding fish were usually tossed onto the bank to die rather than thrown back into the water, the idea being coyotes, hawks, crows or other scavangers would find and dispose of them.

Live bait fishermen still outnumber those who use artificials, but there are many lure and fly fishermen around today who have made the decision to practice catch and release fishing. Today many fishermen catch fish every time they are on the water, and rarely, if ever, take a fish home.

In some places catch and release is prescribed by law, and anglers must return all fish they catch to the water unharmed. In other areas only fish of a certain size may be kept, and in still other places the resource is protected by daily possession limits.

It is usually the trout fisherman who is most strictly limited in the size and number of fish he can kill because of the constantly dwindling amount of quality trout-supporting habitat, the steadily increasing number of fishermen, and the subsequent decline in trout populations and lagging stocking programs.

With the recent skyrocketing popularity of largemouth bass fishing, much of the conservation ethic rubbed off onto bass fishermen, and suddenly catch and release is in, and anyone who lugs home a stringer of dead bass is held in low regard by his fellow bass fishermen.

Attitudes about fishing have changed, both out of awareness and necessity, and on the whole the changes have been good, at least under the conditions we are experiencing today. Fishermen are becoming more aware of, and concerned about, environmental issues, and are more knowledgeable about the fish they enjoy pursuing.

Except in spots where it is strictly regulated by law, catch and release is primarily a personal choice made by the individual fisherman, and some anglers have worked out their own ethics in that regard. I have a friend who loves to fish for trout and bass with fly fishing gear, and he returns every fish he catches to the water. But, when huge schools of white bass are running in Nebraska's large reservoirs, he fishes with spinning gear and takes his full limit of white bass (25 per day) as often as he can get on the water. He doesn't waste the fish – he cleans every one and carefully prepares and freezes each catch so he and his family can enjoy delicious fish suppers nearly every week of the year.

Panfish and bass are ideal adversaries for fly fishermen for a number of reasons. They aren't hard to find, in fact, there are good populations nearly everywhere. They are fun to catch and great on the table.

By virtue of their sheer numbers, there are enough bluegill, crappie and bass to keep fly rodders happy for a long, long time. It's hard to find a pond, lake, reservoir, creek, or river that doesn't have a good number of one or all of these species. The lone exception may be cold water streams that are better suited for trout and their kin, but if you want to fish for bass and panfish, just pick up your gear and go.

There are plenty of panfish for everyone, so if you decide to take a mess of bluegill or crappie home for supper, you can do it without having to wrestle with your conscience. Biologists tell us harvesting a small number of fish has little effect on the overall population, and in fact, may actually help maintain a healthy balance in the lake. Take what you can reasonably use, but avoid being wasteful and make use of what you take.

Bass fishermen seem to be a little more eager to release their fish than pan-fishermen, unless they catch a truly large fish and want to have it mounted for the den or photographed to show their friends. Again, taking an occasional fish, even a large bass, won't upset the population, but removing several large fish each time out from the same body of water can have a detrimental effect.

Fishermen have to be aware that every body of water, regardless of size, has a very delicate balance that must be maintained if it is to be a productive fishery. Biologists refer to that balance as the *predator-prey* relationship: the number of prey fish and the number of predator fish that share the lake. If there are too few prey fish, the predators won't have enough groceries to go around, and they will either not grow to their potential, or nature will reduce their numbers to a manageable level. If there are too few predators, the smaller, more prolific prey fish will overpopulate and become stunted as too many of them compete for a limited amount of forage.

For instance, the predator-prey relationship can easily be demonstrated in an average-sized farm pond. A couple of good bass fishermen who fish the pond several times a month and remove three or four bass on each trip, can easily ruin the pond's fishery. Biologists say the ideal bluegill-largemouth bass relationship in the average farm pond is about 4:1; four pounds of bluegill per each pound of bass in the pond. If both anglers remove two 3-pound bass on each trip (which doesn't seem to be a lot of fish), they should also remove 48 pounds of bluegill each trip to maintain the pond's proper predator-prey relationship.

Obviously, bass fishermen aren't going to remove that many bluegill, in fact, they probably won't take any bluegill at all, which means they don't have to remove too many keeper bass to severely damage the fishery in that small body of water. The bluegill population must be controlled either by fishing or predation by bass. Taking a relatively few large bass during a few trips, can not only deplete the bass population, but can also create a situation in which there are too many bluegill and not enough bass in the pond to control their numbers. That can cause poor fishing for both species.

It is most important that all bass in the 12- to 15-inch size range be returned to the lake in good condition, because they are the right size to effectively control the bluegill population. Bass of that size feed heavily on 4- to 5-inch bluegill and are needed to keep the prolific panfish in check. The 12- to 15-inch bass are also very successful spawners, which helps to ensure that the proper predator-prey relationship is maintained in the pond.

While catch and release is a worthwhile practice in most cases, it does have its limitations. Some fishermen think if the fish they return to the water swims away, it's guaranteed to live a long life, pack on the pounds and be available to fight again another day. Unfortunately, that's not always the case.

The natural tendency when you hook a large fish is to fight it slowly and deliberately, lift it from the water to unhook it, take a good look at it, hold it up for everybody else to see, take a few pictures, then ease it back into the water and let it go. The chances of the fish surviving after being treated in this manner are pretty slim. Even if it swims away and appears to be alright, it may die within a few hours.

If you are going to release fish, do it right! Here's how:

1. Never play a fish to total exhaustion. Biologists say when a fish becomes overly fatigued, chemical changes in its body can cause its death, even though the angler handles it properly after it is landed.

2. Keep the fish in the water as much as possible. It is often easy for a fly fisherman to pluck his fly from the fish's lip without removing the fish from the water at all, or touching it with either hand. To accomplish this on a lightly-hooked fish, grasp the fly between thumb and forefinger and bend and twist the fly downward in one motion, backing the fly out of the fish's lip tissue. This is most easily accomplished with barbless hooks, though it can be done with flies tied on standard hooks. In fact, the fish will often make a final flip as it is being led toward the angler and release itself. That's when the experienced angler smiles and says something like, "Hey, how'd you like that beautiful release?"

3. If the fish must be handled, be sure to wet your hands before touching it. Handling a fish with dry hands can remove the mucous covering that guards the fish against bacterial and fungal infections.

4. Always handle a fish carefully. Don't squeeze it, don't put your fingers into or on its gills, and don't put your fingers in its eye sockets.

5. Fish taken on flies are rarely hooked deep in their mouths or throats. But, if a fish you want to release is deeply hooked, cut the leader as closely to the eye of the hook as possible and leave the hook embedded in the fish rather than trying to force the hook free. The fish may be severely injured if you try to remove the hook, but if you leave it alone, the fish's digestive juices will dissolve the hook in a comparatively short period of time and the fish will have a much better chance of surviving.

6. When you release a fish, lower it gently into the water as quickly as possible after catching it. Cradle it upright in the water with your hand until it has regained its equilibrium. Move the fish back and forth in the water very slowly so water moves across its gills, replenishing oxygen in its body.

7. Treat any fish you catch gently because it deserves your respect. Largemouth bass, smallmouth bass, and crappie can be easily handled by grasping the lower jaw, but a bluegill's mouth is so small it's easier to grasp it across the back. Slide your hand along its back from its head towards its tail so your palm presses the dorsal fin flat against its back, so it doesn't flare the fin and stick your hand.

8. The proper handling and release of a fish is an important basic fishing skill that should be considered to be just as important as learning to hook and play it.

PART II

FLY FISHING TECHNIQUES

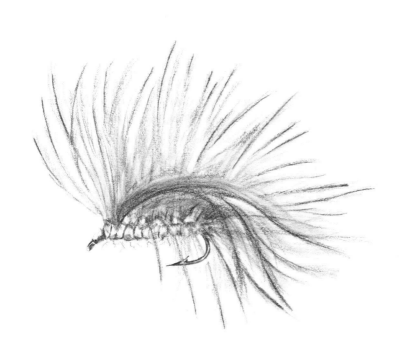

READING A LAKE

Learning how to choose the proper equipment, how to cast, habits of the fish, and how to tie and choose productive patterns are all important parts of fly rodding for panfish and bass, but none of it means much if you aren't able to choose productive areas of the lake to fish.

A good fisherman must acquire the knowledge and develop the skills necessary to look at a body of water and accurately predict where the fish will be located at certain times of the year. That's what we call *reading a lake*.

This is somewhat easier for fly fishermen to do than many other kinds of fishermen, because for the most part, fly fishing for panfish and bass is a shallow water sport. We believe fish relate to specific kinds of structure for logically and biologically sound reasons and most of that structure can be seen in shallow water. A fly fisherman has no need for depth finders unless he's fishing from a boat, and then properly fishing deep water channels, sunken islands and deep water points with a fly rod is a specialized skill not practical or attractive to most fly slingers.

Biologists say the majority of game fish can be found in a relatively small amount of the water in a particular lake at any particular time. In other words, a lot of fishermen waste a lot of time fishing where there aren't any fish to be caught.

The first thing a fly rodder can do when he looks at a lake map or the lake itself, is to immediately eliminate 90 percent of the water area he sees. The water too deep to fish, water that is probably not holding any fish, and water that is too shallow to fish should be ignored.

A contour map can be a big help to a fly fisherman, but because he's mostly interested in areas near the bank, he can determine the bottom contours of an area that looks good to him by doing a little fishing there. Remember, not all of the spots that look good to the fisherman will hold fish, but his odds of catching fish are much higher if he starts fishing where there is appropriate structure.

Lake Map

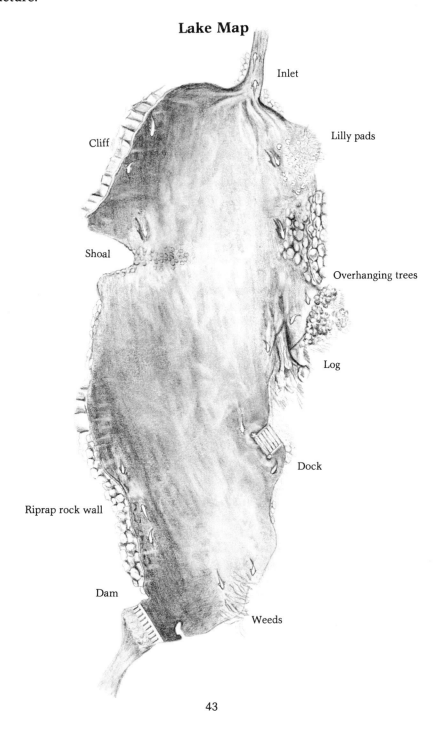

Inlet

Lilly pads

Cliff

Overhanging trees

Shoal

Log

Dock

Riprap rock wall

Dam

Weeds

Everybody talks about structure and it means different things to different people. When we talk about *structure* we mean a combination of two things — any object or contour that breaks up or changes the regular contour of shape of the bottom or surface of a body of water, AND, any edge that leads from shallow water to deeper water.

There is a very important concept that goes hand-in-hand with structure fishing. The concept can be summed up in four words: Fish Follow Structural Routes. That means fish follow various forms of structure to travel from one place to another, and these routes are like roads that lead throughout the lake. Here are some types of structural routes where the fly fisherman should look for fish: treelines, the edges of weedbeds, the edges of submerged creek channels, submerged roadbeds, the face of the dam, and places where shallow water drops off rapidly into deep water.

What this means to the fly rodder is an isolated spot of good cover will be less productive than a similar spot connected to other forms of cover by some sort of structural route. Panfish and bass do not like to travel across large flat areas of water over a barren bottom. They stick to structural routes that offer protection and forage for them while they travel.

Some types of structures are highly visible, anyone can readily see and identify trees, brushpiles, weedbeds, and rocks, but there are some other important things that aren't as obvious, like submerged creek channels, submerged road beds, or rapid drop-offs. Some will have to be located by using a map, others can be found just by fishing the area.

When you see a new body of water for the first time, try to look at it from the highest point around. That may be the top of the dam at a reservoir, a high hill, or even the entry road that winds over high hills leading to the impoundment. From a higher level you can easily see some of the things we are going to discuss.

The most obvious things are right there staring you in the face. You can easily see the country surrounding the lake. In most cases the lake bottom will be similar to the surrounding countryside. If you see a high hill with a steep bank falling into the water, you can be sure it continues to be steep under the water. That means the water will probably be deep and dangerous to wade, though it may be accessible with a float tube or boat.

If you see an old road on one side of the lake that leads into and disappears in the water, look straight across the water and chances are it emerges on the other side. If there is a little valley between two hills along the shoreline, that lower area will probably continue underwater. If the land is relatively flat or slopes gently on the bank, there will probably be a slow slope under the water, maybe even a large flat area. If it is covered with weeds, great! If it's just an expanse of water, it probably should be avoided.

A good bass will turn a float tuber around with its strong runs.

You can easily see inlet areas where streams flow into the lake. You can see submerged treelines and stump fields, large weed beds, rocky areas, the dam itself, boat ramps, coves and brushpiles. All of these spots are important when you are deciding where to fish.

Also be aware that in a reservoir the outlet structure, the spillway constructed on the face of the dam which is used to regulate the impoundment's water level, is built at the point of deepest water along the dam, probably the point where the original creek channel was located. The creek channel travels from the inlet area to the spillway and is an important structural feature of that body of water — fish use it to locate forage and to travel from one point on the lake to another.

Remember too, that late fall in most reservoirs, lakes and ponds, is just the reverse of early spring — the lake is cooling instead of warming, but fish react in much the same way during both seasons. Look for them in late fall in the same areas you found them in the spring. They won't be preparing to spawn, but they'll be in shallow water in the same structural areas looking for comfortable temperatures and food.

INLET AREAS

The inlet areas are very important, especially early in the spring when snowmelt, runoff and spring rains flow into the lake bringing warmer water and food organisms along with it. There are usually willows and cattails or other forms of vegetation in shallow water along the lake banks near the spots where streams flow into the lake and these also hold fish. Take a good look at the inlet area – if it has submerged or partially submerged trees, it will probably be much deeper than an inlet that has no trees.

In late spring and summer some fish travel up the stream channel and stay in deeper water near the mouth of the inlet. Here the water is full of oxygen and the stream carries food to the congregating fish.

During dry periods in late spring and summer, many inlet areas become very shallow with much growing vegetation, stumps, and partially submerged logs and trees. These areas can provide excellent fishing during all but the very hottest periods of the year, though getting to them is frequently very difficult for the fisherman. These marshy areas typically have very soft, mushy bottoms which makes wading extremely difficult; the water is frequently only knee deep, far too shallow for using a float tube; and there are spots where the water is only inches deep and strewn with logs, branches and brushpiles. Getting into those areas, even by canoe or flat-bottomed boat is nearly impossible.

In the late fall, inlet areas again attract fish because the water flowing into the lake is warm while much of the rest of the lake is quickly cooling.

NORTHERN BANKS

These areas are important in the spring because the water warms there before other areas of the lake. The sun shines on the north side for longer periods of the day and stimulates vegetation growth, which attracts small fish and minnows. Bluegill, crappie and bass look at these areas as perpetual lunch counters because they feed on everything from the vegetation itself and the zooplankton associated with it, to the minnows and small fish that are also attracted to the growing vegetation.

TREES

Lines of submerged and partially submerged trees probably indicate the path of the creek channel and the resulting deeper water. Crappie, bass, and bluegill, to some extent, work those treelines looking for food. The crappie and bass are interested in small fish, the bluegill are more interested in insects and grubs associated with the trees.

Trees along the bank, especially those that have branches that hangover or droop into the water, are extremely good fish holding spots for several reasons. They provide shade and cooler water in the summer; they provide hiding spots, both among the branches and in exposed root systems; they provide food by virtue of flying insects that are attracted to the trees and insects that fall from the branches. Minnows utilize zooplankton associated with the vegetation and the minnows attract larger fish; and there is normally not much disturbance along the bank in these areas. The best way to fish these spots is quietly from as far away as possible to avoid disturbing the fish.

Many reservoirs have willows growing on shallow points that extend out into the water. Willows are dynamite fishing spots and all trees that grow in the water create areas of high zooplankton and insect production and that means there will be fish there to feed on them.

STUMP FIELDS

Stump fields are excellent spots to find panfish and bass. These areas produce many forage items, offer protection and provide ambush spots. Fish them slowly and thoroughly. In the summer concentrate casting to the shady sides of the stumps where bass will likely be hiding.

STICK-UPS

Stick-ups are trees and bushes that grow in the water and logs that have fallen into the water. These are usually found in fairly shallow areas, but they provide protection for predator fish and can be very productive in spring and fall.

SUBMERGED ROADBEDS

Submerged roadbeds are important for several reasons. The submerged roadbed will probably be a little higher than the surrounding area and it will typically have ditches on each side. Those ditches are ideal structural routes for fish travel and they provide drop-off areas where the fish can find food being washed across the lake. The surface of an inundated roadbed is usually pretty stable, so it provides a comparatively shallow area where an angler can sometimes wade out into the lake for some distance and cast to the deeper water on either side of the road.

DAMS

The dam is a natural fish holding area. Crappie spawn there in the spring. Moss and algae grow on the rocks and attract insects and small fish, which in turn attract bluegill, crappie and bass. There are frequently small crustaceans and all kinds of critters living in the rocks that attract fish. A good example happened early one spring when the sun was beginning to warm the world after a long, hard winter. It is common to see garter and bull snakes along dam faces, or anywhere around the lake for that matter, but garter snakes in particular are plentiful in the rocks in early spring. I was casting small streamers for crappie one warm spring afternoon and noticed a garter snake swimming along the dam face. As it began crawling out of the water onto a rock, a good-sized largemouth burst from the water and grabbed the snake in its mouth, then fell onto the shallow rocks, flipped a couple of times and disappeared into deeper water with its lunch. It was a thrilling sight, one I've never seen repeated though I'm sure bass eat snakes when they can.

The dam face provides a vertical drop into deep water and gets a lot of wave action, meaning forage items are being constantly swept there and churned under because of the breaking waves. There is deep water in front of the dam, which is cool in the summer and warm in the winter. The submerged creek channel provides a natural structural route to the dam and fish then fan out along the rocky structure.

BOAT DOCKS

If there are boat docks on the lake, be sure to explore them for panfish. They provide shade and security, and are especially attractive during the summer months.

Bluegill Fishing

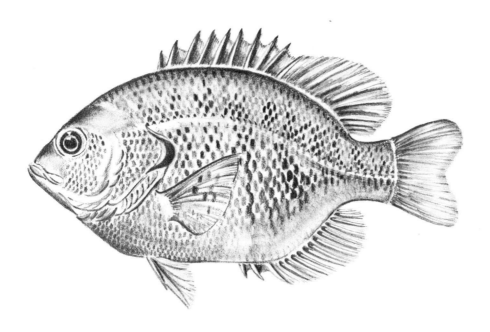

BLUEGILL FISHING

I want to go on record as being a devoted bluegill fisherman. That doesn't mean I fish only for bluegill, because I pursue many species of fish, but it does mean I rank bluegill fishing near the top of the list of things I like to do most.

Bluegill fishing is exciting, it can be extremely challenging, and there is nearly always plenty of action. I've spent much time fishing for many game fish species, and I've enjoyed every hour I've spent on the water, but some of my most favorite memories are of days spent taking bluegill with a fly rod.

Too many people look down their nose at bluegill and think of them as kid's fish because gills were the fish they remember catching when they were young. Later, as they became interested in catching larger fish or more prestigious species, they forgot how much fun they had catching bluegill. Many anglers get away from bluegill fishing for a number of years, then later rediscover them and wonder why they didn't come back to fishing for fun a lot sooner.

I have a friend, Kirk Peters, who is a fisheries biologist with the Nebraska Game and Parks Commission. He is currently assigned to working at the Crawford Fish Hatchery, a state facility that produces brown and rainbow trout for stocking in the streams and lakes of Nebraska's panhandle.

Kirk is surrounded by some great trout waters and does a good amount of trout fishing, but he still has a soft spot in his heart for bluegill. "I think bluegill are special. I'll show people where I fish for trout and take them to the very best areas, but I'll never share my favorite bluegill spots with anybody."

The bluegill is known by different names in different parts of the country. In the South and Southeast they call him bream or brim, in other areas he's known as copperbelly, blue sunfish, or sun perch. Some people who are less enamored with him than I refer to him as *them little fish*.

He is found in abundance in all but two states, Alaska and Maine. In the South where the growing season is long, he may average a pound or better.

No other fish has the heart of a bluegill. He's one of the smallest of all freshwater gamefish, but he has the reputation of being, pound for pound or, more appropriately ounce for ounce, the strongest and most belligerent of them all. The most descriptive remark I've heard about bluegill is, "if he weighed 5 pounds you'd never be able to get him in the boat." It's probably true.

A bluegill knows instinctively how to fight a hook. He uses a number of moves to escape and battles until he is exhausted. The instant he feels the hook he usually tries to escape by running directly away from the fisherman, even if only for a short distance. That only tightens the line and he is invariably jerked off course, so he immediately turns at a right angle and uses the broad flat side of his body to brace against the line and dart in one direction or the other. Then he may dive straight down or head straight up toward the surface. Sometimes he'll run at the line — and the fisherman — for a short distance and sometimes gets enough slack in the line that he dislodges a poorly set hook.

Usually though, he takes the fly so quickly and hard that he hooks himself well and despite his valiant efforts to escape, the fight ends with the fisherman backing the hook from his jaw.

But, that doesn't diminish the effort he puts into trying to escape on his own. He is very determined and fights well in short bursts, like Sugar Ray Leonard throwing a blinding flurry of punches then backing away for a second, only to attack again while his opponent is still off balance and reeling from the first assault.

The bluegill is also a master strategist. No matter how long he fights or how furious the battle, he always saves one last burst of energy for an escape attempt after the hook has been removed an he's being held in the fisherman's hand. Be ready for one final desperate flop — it has frustrated every bluegill fisherman at one time or another and has saved more than a few fish from the frying pan.

There are several sunfish that people lump together under the name bluegill, like the pumpkin seed, green sunfish, and redear sunfish, to name a few. Though some other sunfish species look like the bluegill, and some may even be hybrids, there is only one true species of bluegill.

The bluegill's Latin name is *Lepomis macrochirus*. He is a wide, thin fish with a mouth so small that it severely limits the food he can eat. That information is important to the fly fisherman because it also limits the size of fly used to catch him.

The male is quite colorful, especially in the spring before and during the spawn when his iridescent colors are especially bright and deep. Though there are some color differences between fish in different parts of the country and from waters of varying quality, his back is usually a deep dark olive or dark emerald green. His sides are lighter in color and are usually marked with dark verticle bars. His belly is a dusky white and his breast is a combination of various shades of yellow and reddish-orange. When seen in the sunlight his sides reflect shades of purple, blue and green. The lower part of his gill cover and chin is blue and the entire ear flap, located at the top portion of the gill, is black.

The female's colors are lighter and less striking. She usually has a dark area on her back, and her sides range in color from shades of light yellow and dusky white, and have hints of greens and blues. She also has the distinctive all-black ear flap.

Bluegill aren't large by any means, in fact, the average gill is about 9½ inches long and weighs around 12 ounces. The world record bluegill tipped the scales at only 4 pounds, 12 ounces and was 15 inches long. It was caught by T.S. Hudson, who was fishing Ketona Lake, Alabama, on April 9, 1950.

The bluegill is the most abundant of all sunfishes. He is found in ponds, lakes, reservoirs, and slow moving warmwater streams, creeks and rivers across the country. He prefers warm, clear waters where there are lots of aquatic plants and other kinds of cover, but he can also tolerate waters with high turbidity and siltation.

One of the reasons he is so popular is that he always seems to be hungry and ready for a good tussel. A bluegill is primarily a sight feeder, which means he depends more on his sense of sight to locate food than his sense of smell. His mouth is small, and that means a fisherman will have a better chance of hooking him if he uses a small fly. In most situations bluegill flies should be no larger than size 8 or smaller than size 14. Sure, there are a few stories about a one-half pound bluegill trying to tackle a huge bass plug or a king-size spoon somebody was using to catch northerns. The bluegill is usually hooked on one barb of the treble hook and it does look like the fish really tried to swallow a lure as large as himself, but I'll guarantee you'll catch more bluegill, more often, on small flies.

Young bluegill feed on microscopic zooplankton, tiny water fleas and some types of aquatic vegetation, while adult bluegill can handle bigger prey like nymphs, small crustaceans, mayflies, damselflies, crickets, grasshoppers, worms, and an occasional small fish, though they aren't known to be voracious fish-eaters. They will also occasionally eat a bit of vegetation, especially during summer when finding minnows and insects is a bit more difficult.

This bluegill took weighted McGinty fished in shallow water near tree branches drooping into water.

Bluegill are daylight feeders. Rarely, if ever, will you catch one at night. In the spring and fall when water temperatures are moderate, a fly fisherman can catch 'gills from shallow coves during most of the day, but during the hot summer months fishing is best in the early morning and in the evening until dark. Evening fishing begins as soon as the sun no longer shines directly on the water and a slight drop in temperature occurs.

Mid-afternoon may provide some good fishing action on cool or over-cast summer days, but as a rule-of-thumb, bluegill fishing pretty much shuts down during the hot part of the day.

On those scorching summer days when the temperature climbs well into the 90's by late morning, the fisherman should be on the water early, ready to intercept the 'gills as they move from deeper, cooler water into the shallows to feed. That feeding activity starts shortly after sunrise and may last to mid-morning, depending on when the rising water temperature drives them back to deep water again.

The same movement into shallow water occurs again in the late afternoon or early evening and lasts until dark. A tip for evening fishermen — be sure to carry a can or bottle of insect repellent with you while you're fishing. The bluegill may be biting better than you've ever seen before, and you can bet your float tube the mosquitos will be even more ravenous. Be careful to keep the repellant away from flies and your reel — it may damage the reel's surface and give your flies an unpleasant odor that might be detected by the fish. Use a spray repellant or wash your hands thoroughly after using the liquid, cream or lotion.

Like largemouth bass, bluegill are very cover (structure) oriented. Very seldom will you find them in open water except over a submerged weed-bed that can't be seen from the surface. To find bluegill look for some kind of cover — a thick weedbed, an area of stick-ups, a boat dock, or a pier. Sometimes a submerged brush pile, a bush or tree growing in the water along the shoreline, a point where willows and reeds grow near shore, or an area where there are logs and broken timber in the water will hold fish. The Golden Rule in finding good bluegill fishing is "look for cover."

Some of the most important types of cover are areas of aquatic vegetation, like weedbeds, stands of reeds and cattails, lily pad fields, and submerged areas of thick grass. Aquatic vegetation is very important to bluegill because it provides places for them to hide and escape from predators — places where they can find food, like insects, crustaceans, small minnows and the plants they sometimes consume — and is an excellent source of dissolved oxygen, all necessary for the fish to survive.

BLUEGILL FISHING THROUGH THE YEAR

It's too bad, but some anglers limit their bluegill fishing to the spring because they think bluegill are easiest to locate and catch when they are spawning. Those people are right to a certain extent, the fish are easy to locate and can be easy to catch during the spawn, but there are other times of the year when the fishing is just as good and sometimes even better than in the spring.

Unlike some other species of fish, bluegill stay active all winter. Though their metabolism does slow in cold water, there is really no dormant period during any part of the year. Ice fisherman can tell you bluegill bite well during winter, and large numbers are taken through the ice in those parts of the country where the lakes freeze over.

However, in the northern states where freeze-ups do occur, there is one time of the year when it's tough to catch any bluegill at all. That's the period that starts in the late winter when the ice is too thin to support a fisherman, and ends about the time all of the ice has melted from the lake. There may be open water near shore during part of that period, but for all practical purposes bluegill fishing virtually comes to a halt.

Then, as the number of daylight hours increase, and the spring sun starts warming air and water, bluegill begin moving and feeding again, and another fishing season is underway.

SPRING

I'm always surprised by how quickly water temperatures warm in the spring. It seems like I can be wading or float tubing one day and the water seems very cold, then the very next day it seems to have warmed to a comfortable level. In reality it may not change that quickly at all, but it seems like the lake warms overnight. The point is, when you're waiting for the water in your favorite lake or pond to warm and trigger spring fishing action, check it often, the temperature may rise very quickly. That change can produce good fishing tomorrow even though nothing was biting today.

The best way to get a jump on the season and start fishing as early in the spring as possible, is to get permission to fish a farm pond, or concentrate your efforts on smaller public fishing areas. Water temperatures in those small shallow bodies of water rise more rapidly than in larger, deeper lakes and reservoirs.

In early spring the best fishing will be found in two particular places: at inlets where flowing creek water enters the lake, and in shallow-water coves on the north side of the lake.

Early in the year fishing can be fantastic near the spot where a creek enters the pond or lake. Water flowing into the lake is warmer than water that has been standing in it, and the flowing water brings forage from throughout the watershed into the lake. Bluegill and other fish species, too, position themselves near the inlet and take advantage of items being swept along by the current. It's like a never-ending smorgasbord and is a welcome treat for hungry fish after a winter of slim pickings.

Float tube lets Verl Borg cast to outside edge of weedbed for bluegill.

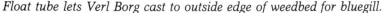

Nice bluegill taken on an Adams Irresistible.

The best spots to fish are along edges of the inlet and the creek channel. Those areas are typically bordered by shallow flats where lots of emergent vegetation grows. Fish lie along the sides of dropoffs waiting for the current to bring a selection of groceries past.

To take bluegill very early in the season, stand on the bank along the creek channel, and cast a size 8 or size 10 weighted black, brown, or dark green Woolly Worm up the creek channel and let the current carry it into the lake. The proper technique is a little tough to get the hang of when you first try it, but with some practice it becomes easy:

1. Strip a good amount of line from the reel to allow for the distance the fly will be carried by the current, as it floats down the creek and into the lake.

2. Make the cast upstream a short distance and try to drop the fly where you can see the current is moving at a decent pace.

3. Keep the line from developing a lot of slack as it floats downstream past you by raising the rod tip and lifting slack line from the water as the fly approaches your position.

4. Slowly lower the rod tip and let out line as the fly is swept past your position and into the lake. Cast upstream far enough that the fly sinks before it enters the lake so its entry appears to be very natural. It shouldn't take you more than a couple of casts to get the hang of it. You'll know you did everything right the first time a big bluegill takes off with your fly.

Some bluegill feed at the creek inlet for a short time and then move out of that area. They move to warmer spots along the north side of the lake, where the spring sun's rays fall for the longest period during the day, and quickly warm the shallow water there. That warmer water is not only more comfortable for the fish, it also causes aquatic vegetation to begin growing, which provides a ready food supply for the bluegill.

This warm shallow water is a good place to try your Girdle Bugs and Lightning Bug flies. Use the unweighted styles, cast them near standing grasses and weeds, and let them sink slowly in the water. A slow retrieve will work better this early in spring than a fast one, so try to limit it to short jerks of 4 to 5 inches and pause a few seconds between each jerk.

Fish are extremely nervous at this time of year, so careful, deliberate wading is essential. Loud noises and sudden movement will drive fish out of the shallows and may make them so cautious they won't resume feeding for some time.

Casting along a weed edge is much more productive if you cast parallel to shore rather than at right angles to it because parallel casts keep the fly in shallow water throughout the whole retrieve where fish are most likely to be. Casting toward the weeds and retrieving the fly into deeper water, allows the fly to be shallow for only a short portion of the cast. Make your casts as close as possible to the weeds at first, then progressively work deeper water further from shore until you locate the fish. Use the countdown method to find the proper depth as you work your casts slowly into deeper water.

Mother Nature induces fish to feed heavily in the spring as a means of providing nourishment that will see them through the rigors of the coming spawn. The female fish needs plenty of food to nourish thousands of eggs developing in her body, and males have to sock away some groceries for the hard work of building a nest and defending it and their offspring from predators.

It isn't long until the water temperature climbs into the high 50's and low 60's, and the bluegill begin preparations for spawning. Warming temperatures cause the males to head for shallow water to find suitable nest sites, while the ladies congregate in deeper water waiting for nest construction to be completed. A male never seems to be in much of a hurry to pick a spot − or maybe he is just very particular − but the process of selecting the right site may take a week or more. During that period he makes several trips from deep water to shallow each day, apparently searching trips from deep water to shallow each day, apparently searching for just the right location.

He eventually locates a suitable spot where the bottom is sand or gravel and he hollows out a depression 12 to 24 inches wide with his tail. Most often the chosen spot will be in direct light, but it may also be shaded by trees during parts of the day. Generally a number of bluegill beds will be found in the same area.

After the bed is formed, the male hovers above it and periodically sweeps it clean with his tail. When the water temperature rises to about 67 degrees the female moves onto the bed and lays her eggs. The male fertilizes the eggs and stays at the bed to protect them while the female drifts back into deeper water. After a short recuperation period she moves to shallow areas where she feeds on aquatic grasses and weeds and rests undisturbed while regaining her strength.

The eggs hatch in 2 to 5 days. The male keeps the young fish corralled in the bed and continues to guard them from predators for several more days.

Bedding areas can be spotted from the shore, or from a boat, and finding them is pretty easy if you wear polarized glasses. Some veteran bluegill fishermen say they can smell a spawning area by walking along the bank. The smell is distinctive musky, fishy odor and some fishermen's noses are so sensitive to it they can find a bedding spot as easily as a pointer can locate a covey of quail. Another method is to watch for spots where bubbles are caused by gases being released from the lake bottom when the male fans sand and gravel with his tail and are a sure sign of bluegill activity.
the male fans sand and gravel with his tail and are a sure sign of bluegill activity.

A male bluegill can easily be taken on weighted flies during the spawn, not because he is hungry, but because he is determined to keep intruders away from his nest. One afternoon I watched the activity at a spawning area for some time, interested in how persistently the males guarded their nests. I threw an unhooked garden worm into one of the beds and watched while the male darted at it, picked it up in his mouth and carried it away from the bed, then dropped it and hurried back to his station. Any other time he would have consumed that worm in a single gulp.

A bluegill reacts the same way when a fly enters his area. He'll strike at it to drive it away and if that doesn't work he'll take it in his mouth to move it. Once it's in his mouth all you have to do is set the hook and play the fish. A size 8 weighted yellow, green or brown Woolly Worm or size 10 weighted Girdle Bug fished in bedding areas will help you to quickly fill your fish basket with bluegill.

A few days after the fry hatch they are large and strong enough to adequately fend for themselves, so the male leaves the spawning area. He heads for deeper, cooler water to rest and feed while recovering from those long days of protecting his spawning area and the fry. Fly fishermen can take advantage of the fish's returning appetite by using wet flies and nymphs in the deeper water near submerged weedbeds or grassy flats. A size 10 or size 12 Black Gnat, Improved McGinty wet fly or Gold-Ribbed Hare's Ear nymph are good choices for this situation. Use weighted versions of these patterns with a wet-tip fly line to get the fly down fast and keep it deep during the retrieve. A few of the fish slip back into shallow water during early morning and late afternoon to feed, but the majority of them remain offshore in deeper water throughout the day during the post-spawn period.

After a few days of recuperating in deep water, groups of males disperse and move to the grassy, weedy areas where the females have been waiting and resume their normal early summer activities.

When the males move away from their nests, the newly hatched bluegill join other groups of fry, form large schools and stay in shallow water where there is plenty of aquatic vegetation where they hide and feed on zooplankton, tiny water fleas and the new vegetation.

The ideal time for bluegill fishing is from the end of the spawn until the beginning of hot summer because the fish spend nearly all day feeding in shallow water. It's a good time to use unweighted Girdle Bugs, which float on the surface awhile before they become water-logged and sink. A Girdle Bug is a good fly for determining if the fish are ready to begin surface feeding without committing yourself to using a dry fly pattern that can be fished only in one manner.

This period is what we refer to as "freezer-filling time" because it is one of the two best times of the year for bluegill fishing and is the ideal time for collecting enough bluegill fillets to provide delicious meals throughout the year. Be on the water every chance you get during this period, even if it's only for an hour or so after work. In additin to being an outstanding time to fish, it's also a great way to unwind after a tough day at the office.

SUMMER

As spring turns to summer, the days get longer, hotter, and more humid, and the fish change their daily routine. They spend the hottest parts of the day in deeper, cooler water or in the shade of submerged weedbeds, and then move into shallow water in late afternoons and evenings to feed. If it is really hot, that movement can be relatively slow, and often the action doesn't pickup until 8 or 9 pm. During these times fish stay in shallow water only as long as the temperatures are relatively moderate, which may be only an hour or so.

Excellent examples of largemouth bass and bluegill habitat.

To be successful during midsummer, try fishing early in the morning where weeds and grass grow in shallow water. Start with a size 10 or size 12 McGinty or Black Gnat wet fly to locate fish quickly. Always approach the spot by getting into the water a good distance away and moving as slowly and as quietly as possible to avoid disturbing the fish. Begin casting from a good distance and don't get any closer to the area the fish are using than is necessary.

If you happen to be on the lake during one of those infrequent cooler summer days that sometimes occur after a long period of scorchers, try using a size 12 or size 14 Adams Irresistible dry fly. Cast it as close to cover or vegetation as possible to imitate an insect that has fallen from the weeds and is floating in the water. Depending on the weather conditions you may have fast-paced bluegill fishing for an hour or so, or the action may last only a few minutes. It's in your best interest to play the percentages – when you catch one fish from an area, continue to fish there. Bluegill like company, so when you catch one fish from a particular spot, odds are there are others where that one came from.

There is a small cove on the east side of Pawnee Lake, just a few minutes' drive from Lincoln, Nebraska, that is fairly shallow, and has abundant weed growth along the entire shoreline. The slender trunk of a long-dead tree protrudes from the water in the middle of the cove, maybe 10 to 12 yards from shore. My son Jim and I found the cove early one summer morning and thought it looked like a good bluegill spot. We experimented with several fly patterns, tried fishing several spots around the cove and enjoyed catching a few fish. Then Jim cast a weighted size 10 Improved McGinty wet fly at the tree trunk. Jim is a pretty accurate caster, and the fly landed just inches from the spot where the tree sticks out of the water. The fly slowly sank below the surface and a couple of seconds later BANG! He had a fish. It was a good-sized bluegill and gave Jim a spirited tussel before he finally landed it.

He put the fish in his basket, cast at the tree again and caught another bluegill. After he had landed his fifth or sixth fish on nearly as many casts, I decided to try that spot too, and started casting to the tree from the opposite side of the cove.

If my cast landed within a few inches of the tree I could nearly count on a strike, but if I missed the mark and my fly landed more than a couple of feet away, nothing happened.

We took several more fish from that spot, and then decided to try another place on the lake we always liked to fish. We returned to that cove several more times during summer and fall that year, and always caught fish, though the action never matched the fishing we found that first morning. Sometimes the dead tree trunk would hold fish; sometimes we'd find them near vegetation along the shoreline; sometimes they were in an emergent weedbed off the cove's north shore. They weren't always in exactly the same spot, but we always found them somewhere in the small cove.

We fished that small cove many times in the following 4 or 5 years until Jim enrolled in college in another state. I've located other good bluegill fishing spots and haven't returned to that cove since the last time Jim and I fished it. One day when our schedules allow a fishing trip or two, we'll fish it again and I'm sure we'll find plenty of hungry bluegill waiting, probably in the same spots we fished years ago.

You can catch bluegill right through the heat of the day, even during the hottest part of the summer, if you can locate a weedbed submerged in water at least 3 feet deep. The water does not have to be very deep, in fact, most weedbeds used by bluegill are found in 12 feet of water or less. During summer, extreme heat can cause a loss of dissolved oxygen in some parts of the lake. When the percentage of dissolved oxygen in the water is low, fish move to other parts of the lake where it is higher.

Weeds absorb carbon dioxide and return oxygen to the water, making weedbeds the most oxygen-rich areas in the lake, and consequently, a comfort zone for fish. Weeds provide shade from direct sunlight and water temperatures there are cooler. Weedbeds also attract and produce insects and vegetation bluegill eat, making it an ideal spot for fish to spend the summer months.

To catch fish from submerged weedbeds, cast weighted Woolly Worms, weighted wet flies like the Improved McGinty, and weighted Girdle Bugs along the deep water side of the bed, and retrieve them erratically to entice the fish.

Boat docks and bridges provide constant shade, plus algae and moss grow on the posts or pilings. Bluegill use the shade of these structures to avoid direct sunlight and feed on insects associated with the algae and moss, as well as the vegetation itself.

To best take advantage of bridges and boat docks, cast wet flies or Girdle Bugs into the shade beside and under the dock. Allow the fly to sink awhile before starting the retrieve, then retrieve it in short, erratic spurts. Sometimes boat docks and bridges produce excellent midday bluegill fishing and are certainly worth exploring with a floating/sinking line and weighted flies.

Even during the dog days of summer many fish move to shallow water in the evening to try to scare up a free meal. There are always plenty of insects available in the evening, and fish get into the habit of taking them from the surface. If you are fishing and see activity on the surface, tie on a dry fly and get in on the action.

As summer wears on, grasshoppers, crickets and other terrestrial insects appear everywhere at once. Many are blown or fall into the water and are quickly consumed by fish. Bluegill love all types terrestrial insects, so if you've noticed that grasshoppers and crickets are out, try using a size 10 or size 12 Sponge-bodied Bug and a size 10 or size 12 Letort Cricket. The Sponge-bodied Bug will float on the surface forever while its thin rubber legs jiggle and vibrate seductively. The Letort Cricket floats well and is so light each tiny ripple in the water gives it action.

Because most terrestrial insects are blown or fall into the water from vegetation growing along the shore, cast to places where insects would normally land if that happened, because those spots are the places where fish will be looking for a free meal.

AUTUMN

When water temperatures start cooling in the fall, fish scatter all over the lake, but also spend more time in shallow water than they did during the summer. This is a good time to use Improved McGintys, Black Gnats and Woolly Worms to entice the fish. Dry flies may take a few fish in the evenings, but wet flies will consistently outproduce drys at this time of year. There is one exception to that rule, a dynamite pattern known as the Deerhair Popper.

Fly casting from small boat is a worthwhile tactic, though it takes practice to cast from sitting position.

I'm not sure what a bluegill thinks that popper is — maybe a small frog, maybe a big moth, maybe...well, who knows for sure? But I do know it puts a lot of bluegill in my fish basket. It is especially effective during warm, cloudy, or overcast fall evenings when there is little wind. Cast the Deerhair Popper to shallow water where there are stick-ups or lots of short weeds, and let it lay for a few seconds. Then twitch the popper or jerk it forward to make it "pop" and make bubbles on the water's surface. Hold the rod tightly because you're apt to be treated to a quick, hard strike.

In late fall when water temperatures are falling, bluegill spend a good amount of time in deep water. But, just like in the spring, they can also be found near stream inlets where warm flowing water brings food organisms into the lake.

The key to locating fish in the fall is to think of autumn as a second spring. There won't be a spawn in the fall, but fish will return to the same areas they used prior to the spawn in the spring. Look for them in those spots and use the same flies and techniques that took fish between ice-out and the beginning of the spawn.

As water temperatures continue to fall, fish spend less and less time in the shallows, both because of the lack of forage found there late in the year, and also because deeper water areas are warmer and more comfortable.

FINDING FISH:
Consider the season:

SPRING — right after ice-out fish are scattered.

PRE-SPAWN — near inlets and in shallow water with shoreline vegetation.

SPAWN — shallow, sandy, gravelly water, sometimes in or near lots of weeds.

AFTER SPAWN — (and during the heat of midsummer) deeper water during the day; weedy shallows early and late in the day. Look for deep water weedbeds, deep drop-offs along steep banks, shady cool spots.

EARLY FALL — when temperatures have cooled, bluegill are found all over the lake, in both shallow and deep areas.

LATE FALL — when water is getting cooler, fish will be found in depths, but like spring can be found by stream inlets where incoming water is warmer and brings food organisms into the lake with it.

Crappie Fishing

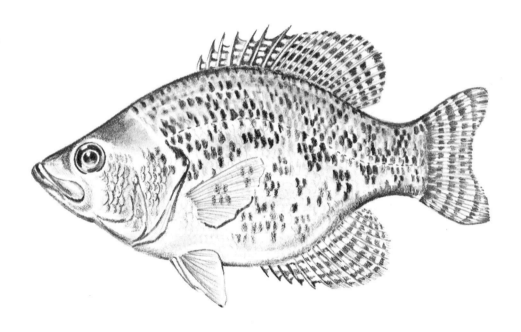

CRAPPIE FISHING

Crappie are among the most popular of all freshwater game fish. They are found from southern Canada to northern Mexico and in every one of the lower 48 United States. They provide excellent fishing opportunities across the country.

There are actually two types of crappie: the white crappie *(Pomoxis annularis)* and the black crappie *(Pomoxis nigromaculatus)*.

Both types look very much alike. Both are deep, slab-sided fish with large mouths, large eyes and an overall silvery sheen. Both species congregate in large schools and both are favorites of fly fishermen because they provide plenty of exciting action and taste great at the table.

WHITE CRAPPIE

The white crappie is known by a number of names in different parts of the country, including papermouth, calico bass, white perch and Sac-a-lait. His back is usually a dark olive to greenish-gold with bluish green, purple and silvery reflections. He has mottled brown and black markings that form narrow vertical bars down his sides. He usually seems to be a bit more elongated than a black crappie of the same age and weight, and is paler in color.

White crappie are found primarily in reservoirs, sand pits and ponds. They can tolerate murky, warm, shallow waters better than their cousins, and are attracted to areas of standing timber, brush, abundant vegetation and stained water.

BLACK CRAPPIE

Black crappie also answer to a variety of names, including calico bass, strawberry bass, speckled perch, and bream. The black's back is the same dark olive to greenish-gold as the white's, and he also has bluish-green, purple and silvery reflections. The black's sides are darker, more heavily speckled and he generally appears to be a bit shorter and stockier than the white crappie of comparable age and weight.

Some black crappie have been stocked in reservoirs, lakes and farm ponds across the country, but they are found in greatest numbers in tidal rivers and brackish waters along both coasts. Black crappie prefer cooler, clearer, deeper waters than whites and do well in natural lakes and reservoirs that have some vegetation, loam, and bottoms with lots of sand and gravel.

Unless otherwise indicated, when we refer to crappie in this book, we'll be talking about both the black and white crappie.

FISHING FOR CRAPPIE

The only shade to be found anywhere on the 280 acre sand pit was at the far edge of one deep cove where several large cottonwoods lined the bank. Some of the trees' heavy leaf-laden branches hung low over the water as much as 9 or 10 feet from shore.

It was one of those scorching mid-summer mornings when just standing in the sun makes your skin hurt. I remember thinking about how warm the water felt on my feet, as I stood ankle deep in the lake and tied a small streamer to my leader tippet.

I had some real reservations about spending an hour in the blazing Midwest August sun, casting to crappie in water about the temperature I usually use for taking a bath. But, J.J. Fairchild said he was going to prove we could catch crappie on flies when everybody else on the lake was sitting on their screened-in porches sweating and drinking lemonade or gin and tonics. Whenever J.J. Fairchild says anything about crappie fishing, I listen closely, because he's the best crappie fisherman I've ever met.

A lot of people find J.J. a little difficult to understand because he's a reluctant transplant from the deep south – I mean REAL deep south – and he doesn't talk in complete sentences like most people, he just mutters a pertinent word or two and lets you fill in the blanks.

I can't remember the entire conversation word-for-word, but his invitation to fish the Nebraska sand pit where he has a summer home went something like this: "crappie bitin'...streamers...good un's...be waitin'...c'mon up."

J.J.'s wife, Carolyn, is the only reason he ever left Mississippi. She inherited the controlling interest in a successful Nebraska corporation from her folks and moved to the Cornhusker state so she could keep tabs on what was happening with her company.

About all J.J. has to do anymore is fish — after growing up in Mississippi he just naturally loves crappie and catfishing. "Fish cats at night...crappie days," he explains.

I don't want to give the impression J.J.'s a hick, in fact, he has a masters degree in accounting. But, now that he doesn't have to keep books anymore, he's just laid back, slow, and determined to enjoy his life doing the things he likes — and the things he likes best are catfish and crappie fishing.

Anyway, J.J. said we could catch crappie on small weighted streamers, even in the intense heat, if we cast them up under the overhanging cottonwood branches where they were feeding on insects and small minnows.

J.J. had a small gray Woolly Bugger, about a size 10, on his line and was false casting toward the cottonwoods. His line flicked back and forth in a tight loop and when he figured he had enough line out, he dropped the rod nearly parallel to the water and shot his fly up under the tree's branches with a powerful sidearm cast.

He stripped the line back in 10-inch increments and bellowed "huuup" when he hooked a fish and "look it...good fish...dive" he grunted as he fought the fish. Then a couple of minutes later he managed "Hey!" and hooked its lip with his thumb and lifted it from the water. The crappie looked like it would weigh a bit over a pound. He dropped it in his fish basket and smiled triumphantly as he checked the condition of his streamer. "There...go on" he invited and stepped back so I could cast without worrying about hitting him.

I cast my Silver Minnow into the shade under the overhanging tree limbs and dropped it in shallow water as close to the bank as I could. I imitated the retrieve J.J. used and had a strike but missed setting the hook. I cast again to the same spot but had no takers. Then, on the third cast, I dropped the streamer in shallow water where a limb actually touched the surface and hooked a fish before I even started my retrieve. The fish fought well and when I lifted it from the water, it looked like a twin of the one J.J. caught minutes before.

J.J. moved to the far side of the trees and I stayed where I was so we were out of each other's way. We continued to catch crappie throughout the morning until I noticed my arms were beginning to look like a medium-rare T-bone steak. We reluctantly left the lake and carried our heavy fish baskets across the parched sand to his cabin.

We drank iced tea, cleaned fish and talked about summertime fly fishing. In his verbal shorthand J.J. taught me a lot about hot weather crappie fishing.

He has fished and studied that particular sand pit for several years and knows it like the grip on his fly rod. He knows there are grass and aquatic vegetation growing in the shallows in that cove and knows the cottonwoods spread their long limbs out over the water providing welcome shade and forage for minnows all summer long. The crappie know that too and stay in the cove where finding grub is easy.

Areas like these are best fished with weighted streamers, long leaders, and floating lines. The idea is to use a streamer that is about the same size and color as the minnows crappie are accustomed to finding and fish it as realistically as possible.

We made our casts at about a 15 degree angle to the shoreline to keep our streamers in water where we thought the fish were most likely to be. It's always best to make your casts parallel to cover where your fly will be seen by the largest number of fish during the longest part of the retrieve.

A weighted fly allows you to control the depth of the streamer by simply varying the speed of the retrieve. A fairly fast retrieve in shallow water keeps the fly near the surface. Slowing the retrieve as the fly moves into deeper water allows it to sink further below the surface. A weight-forward floating line is easy to cast and gives the control to make accurate sidearm casts which are necessary to place your fly under overhanging tree limbs.

J.J. knows crappie head for more comfortable deeper water during hot weather but he also knows they choose deeper water near spots where there is a chance to pick up an easy meal. That's why he can catch crappie during the hottest times of the year in shaded shallow water.

Crappie, like most predator species, spend a great deal of their time pursuing food. Though they school in large groups and often suspend at various depths, they are not really classified as being open-water fish. Their bodies are kind of elongated and flattened, which lets them squeeze into different kinds of cover to hide from larger predators and ambush unsuspecting small protein-rich threadfin and gizzard shad, and other kinds of minnows that congregate in the aquatic vegetation.

Crappie would rather eat fish than other critters, but the size of the fish is very important. They generally utilize small, young-of-the-year or older fish less than about 3 inches long. After a threadfin or gizzard shad grows much longer than 3½ inches, it is too large for the crappie to utilize. Keep that in mind when you are tying streamers for crappie fishing. Make the overall length of the streamer somewhere between 1½ to 2½ inches long, or about hook size 6 to 12. It's OK to make a few streamers shorter than 1½ inches, but don't go longer than about 3 inches.

Minnow size is so important that Morrie Davidson, a dyed-in-the-wool crappie fisherman who uses only minnows year-round, will stand in a bait shop and hand-pick his minnows according to size rather than allow the shop owner to just dip a variety of sizes into his bucket. He says it's important that the bait a crappie sees at first glance is just right, so the fish will hit it out of reflex rather than following and thinking about it for a while. A reflexive strike means more hits and more fish in the basket at the end of the day.

Because of the placement of their eyes, crappie are adept at locating forage which appears at their eye level or above and they don't feed along the bottom a great deal. So, it stands to reason you'll take more crappie if you keep your streamer moving 2 to 3 feet above the bottom rather than letting it bounce along in the sand or mud.

Because crappie hold at various depths, sometimes a little deeper than bluegill and bass, it is important that the fly fisherman be able to locate their position. One way to do that is to cast a weighted streamer on a floating/sinking line, and count off the seconds you allow the fly to sink before starting your retrieve. This is called the count-down method and it's a good one for putting your fly at the same depth for each cast.

To use the countdown method, cast and then let the fly sink while you count one, one hundred – two, one hundred – three, one hundred – four, one hundred and so on before beginning your retrieve. If you get a strike, let the fly sink that far on the next cast. If not, cast and allow it to sink for more counts before starting your retrieve. Remember, crappie are schooling fish, so where you catch one, there are likely to be many more waiting for your streamer.

In open water crappie often suspend at levels where they can feed on large masses of zooplankton or schools of young shad or other minnows. When you are fishing keep in mind that some types of zooplankton are very sensitive to light and move up and down in the water column depending on light conditions – in the bright sunlight they descend in the water column and rise to the surface in the dark. Try to keep your fly in deeper water when the sun is bright, and closer to the surface during low light conditions.

Like most predator fish, crappie are sight feeders and are sensitive to light, which means they prefer low light situations to bright daylight under any circumstances. In stained water you can sometimes catch crappie from shallow water during daylight hours, but if the water is very clear, you'll find the best fishing at dawn, dusk, or at night. If you are lucky enough to be able to fish on an overcast day, you should have decent fishing throughout the entire day regardless of water clarity.

In the spring, crappie move into coves and small bays as soon as ice melts from the lake to feed on minnows and young fish that are attracted to the warm water by blooming microscopic plankton.

The first warm spring days draw crappie to shallow water with the promise of finding plenty of forage. This is a great time to be on the lake with a pair of waders, a fish basket and an assortment of small streamers.

There is a fairly narrow creek, one just wide enough that you can't safely jump across it, that flows into one of my favorite Midwestern reservoirs. As soon as the weather warms to the point where it is comfortable to fish in jeans and a T-shirt, I head for that particular creek. Just a couple of hundred yards from the point where it widens to form one arm of the reservoir, the creek starts a series of "S" bends. On the outside curve of one of those bends there are some stumps and bushes in the water and the branches of trees growing on the bank hang out low over the water.

It's an excellent spot for early season crappie fishing. I never let a spring go by without spending a couple of afternoons there casting streamers near the stumps and bushes. The Black Ghost is a good early season pattern in this particular creek, (and many others across the country) and I like to stand on the bank near the edge of that bend and cast across it so my streamer moves along the outside edge of the stumps and bushes. I cast as closely as possible to the structure and retrieve my streamer past it in a series of erratic darting movements that give hungry crappie the impression it's a wounded minnow and an easy snack.

During this "pre-spawn period" crappie congregate in the general vicinity of areas where they'll later build their nests. In some lakes that may be near a deep water weedbed or along an underwater drop-off. In large reservoirs they use areas with submerged and partially submerged trees standing along the edges of underwater creek channels, while in a small pond or lake they may stack up in an area where there is deep water or one with several kinds of physical structure.

As the water warms in the spring, crappie move near shore where they stay until they've finished spawning. We use floating/sinking lines at this time of year because the fish may be anywhere from 2 to 10 feet deep around submerged brush and other cover, or in open water in narrow bays.

Cast and use the countdown method to explore various depths while retrieving the streamer slowly. Try using a series of slow, steady strips of the line and if that doesn't work, try a series of short pulls and pauses. Try counting to 5 while the first cast sinks, 10 for the second, 15 for the third and so on, until you locate the fish. If you don't find fish easily, move to another spot. Crappie will nearly always bite, so the fly fisherman's problem is just finding where they are congregated.

Verl Borg strikes lightly because crappie have very tender mouths.

Bucktails, streamers and hair-wing trout-type flies are all good choices for early season crappie fishing. Among our favorite colors (and the fishes' as well) are: black, blue, black and orange, black and yellow, red and white, red and yellow, blue and yellow. Start with a large streamer, say a size 6 and if you are not successful try the same pattern in a smaller size. A size 12 bucktail or streamer is as small as we use, though we occasionally use dry flies as small as size 16 for crappie.

Warming water causes crappie to become restless and when the temperatures begin to nudge to mid-50's, the males begin selecting nesting sites. They like spots in coves where the bottom is covered with sand or gravel, clay, muck and various other types of debris. They prefer these spots especially when they are in conjunction with brush, stump fields, weedbeds, or other kinds of aquatic vegetation. Sometimes they spawn on rockpiles and rocky damfaces shortly after walleye complete their spawning activities in the same locations. The guys who know crappie best say the fish tend to spawn deeper than other panfish, and that the larger crappie spawn both earlier and deeper than smaller fish, though they still require the same type of spawning habitat.

The first day or so after they move into their spawning areas, they are a little skiddish and must be approached very cautiously; but as they become more acquainted with the area they loose much of that caution and become very aggressive. When they begin fanning-out nest sites they will actually feed little during the spawn. Crappie are very easy to catch during this period, and fishermen are wise to limit the number of adult fish they take during the spawn.

Under normal conditions a floating line with a 7½ or 9-foot leader and an unweighted streamer is a good combination to catch shallow water spawners. If they are in somewhat deeper water, we recommend using a weighted streamer so the fly goes deep quickly. If spawning occurs in water 10 feet deep or more, or in deep water where there is a lot of wood — submerged trees, stumps, or partially submerged trees — we recommend using a floating/sinking line and weighted fly to put the streamer down where the fish can find it. The floating/sinking line and weighted fly are less likely to be blown or pushed off course by the current, which will help eliminate the chance of being hung-up on every cast.

The actual spawn begins when water temperatures climb above 60 degrees. Crappie nests have been found in water as shallow as 2 feet and as deep as 24 feet — the clarity of the water usually being the determining factor. In clear water they spawn much deeper than in stained or dark water.

Once nest building is completed, females visit the nests and lay their eggs, then slowly move away from the beds to deep drop-off areas and search for food. Males stay on the nests to fan and oxygenate the eggs, and to protect newly hatched fish (fry) from predators until they move away from the nests on their own.

When males leave the spawning beds they join the females along drop-offs or near submerged weedbeds, where both sexes rest and recuperate from the rigors of spawning. During this period they feed occasionally, but because they congregate in deep water and are not feeding very aggressively fishing can be difficult and slow.

As water temperatures climb into the mid-70's there is a lot going on in the lake as normal spring and summer activities get underway. Occasionally crappie are moving across flat shallow areas of the lake, but the most consistent action will occur along submerged creek channel edges, in timbered spots, and in or near beds of aquatic vegetation.

During late spring and early summer crappie feed on insects, larva, and small minnows throughout the day. Weighted Mickey Finn bucktails and Gray Ghost streamers are usually very productive at this time of year because crappie love to feed on small, easy to catch minnows.

The gaudy yellow and red Mickey Finn is an excellent pattern to use during early summer, especially after a rainfall when runoff makes the water murky.

Springtime in the Midwest is commonly wet and windy. Heavy spring rains wash fertile topsoil from farmlands throughout the watershed and creeks and streams carry it into lakes and ponds, turning them the color of medium-strong coffee. Visibility in badly stained water is often as little as 2 or 3 inches. To add to the problem, ever-present spring winds keep the water stirred-up, preventing sediment from sinking to the bottom.

When the water is badly stained fly fishermen should fish near cover where the fish will be holding, and use larger, darker patterns close to the surface because large, dark flies are easier for fish to see silhouetted against the lighter-colored sky. Though the Mickey Finn isn't a dark-colored streamer, the combination of red and yellow materials are apparently fairly easy to see in murky water.

In late spring and early summer, particularly on calm evenings or during periods of warm drizzle, crappie sometimes feed on the surface. That's an ideal time to use a floating line and floating girdle bugs. Cast to weeds, brush, rocks, or debris in the water. Let your bug lie motionless a few seconds, then gently pop it a few inches. When a fish inhales your fly, strike quickly but gently — crappies have tender mouths.

During the mid-summer, crappie fishing gets pretty tough in most areas of the lake. To be successful, you must fish cooler areas, like spots where some kind of structure creates shade on the water, large submerged weedbeds, deep-water holes or submerged creek channels.

If you learn just one thing from reading this book, it should be the most important key to fishing standing waters – weedbeds and brush piles hold fish! Most fishermen know crappie can be difficult to locate during summer, but if you remember to concentrate your efforts on submerged weedbeds, you'll be eating crappie fillets for supper while most other fishermen are eating peanut butter sandwiches.

You may have to fish right among the weeds to hook your fish, or you may find them suspended in deeper water a short distance away, but the basic rule always applies: "find a weedbed and you'll find crappie nearby."

Crappie often patrol the bed's edges in the morning and evening, and sometimes hide in the weeds during the day where the water is cooler and has a high oxygen concentration. Cutouts in dense portions of the bed and holes in the dense weed growth are good places to drop and jig a weighted streamer, like a Silver Minnow, at various depths to pick up a strike.

Many small lakes, reservoirs and river oxbows stay fairly dark during most of the year and the best tactic a fly fisherman can use is to fish larger, darker streamer patterns slowly near the surface so crappie will have a good chance to see them. For instance, try using an unweighted number 8 Black Ghost Bucktail or a black or purple Woolly Bugger, and retrieve it as slowly as possible while keeping it near the surface. Use short jerks to make the fly dart for a couple of inches, then let it hover or move forward very slowly between jerks. In stained water the fish need every opportunity and advantage you can create to help them find and catch the fly.

Many lakes and ponds remain pretty murky throughout the year making darker patterns more successful than streamers with neutral colors.

If you fish stained water a good portion of the time, it is well worth your effort to tie some streamers and bucktails using all black materials.

Many Midwestern lakes and ponds I fish are dirty during much of the year, so I carry a selection of all-black streamers and bucktails in my vest. I tie three patterns, the Woolly Bugger, the Black Ghost, and the Muddler Minnow with all black materials in sizes 6, 8, and 10. I've tested them when the water is very murky by switching back and forth between a black fly and the same pattern tied with regular materials and colors, and I've found the black flies often produce fish while regular color combinations go begging.

In lakes where stained water is not a constant consideration, fly fishermen should make a habit of fishing as many different kinds of cover as they can find. Never pass up flooded timber where it lines the banks of submerged creek channels, stump fields, or spots where trees or other objects on the bank create shade on the water.

The key to consistently successful crappie fishing is think cover. If you can find a shallow flat, with 4 to 5 feet of water and a large amount of arrow-head, smartweed, coontail, or other aquatic vegetation, it's likely there will be a good number of crappie hiding there.

Breaklines are important fish-holding areas that are easily accessible to fly fishermen. Breaklines are edges, those places where one type of structure merges with another type. For instance, breaklines are areas where the shoreline meets the water; where a very rocky bottom becomes sandy; or the edge created by shallow water dropping-off into deeper water. In other words, look for a change in structure.

In natural lakes a very important and productive late-season breakline area is the first major change from shallow to deeper water. During the early fall, crappie sometimes suspend just off the drop-off along the edge of a shallow flat, and flyrodders who use floating/sinking lines and work small streamers along the drop-off can enjoy some fast-paced fishing.

In late fall when the water is rapidly cooling, days are getting noticeably shorter, and overcast days are becoming more frequent, fly fishermen can still take crappie by casting streamers along the face of the dam.

A perfect late fall day for fishing the dam is one which is overcast and the wind is pounding waves on the face of the dam. The wave action warms the water a little along the dam and the waves carry forage into the rocks. Min-nows and small fish move into the rocks to feed on those food organisms, and crappie patrol the dam face to feed on the small fish.

A productive technique to use in this situation is to wade into the water at one end of the dam and cast a weighted streamer parallel to the structure. Start making your retrieves very near the damface, then work out away from the rocks toward the main part of the lake until you find the fish. It can be a lengthy process because you have to cast different distances from the dam as well as making retrieves at various depths. But, once you locate the fish you'll be able to enjoy an afternoon of good fishing.

Crappie will also be associated with weedbeds during the late season, but as the vegetation begins to die they leave the bed and suspend in open water, occasionally moving into the shallows to feed. As the vegetation decays, the process uses oxygen and returns carbon dioxide back to the water. The increased amount of carbon dioxide drives fish from the area.

Fly fishing for crappie is a sport that warms the hearts of tackle and fly manufacturers. Because crappie love to hang around submerged brush, trees and bushes, you often have to put your streamer right in the middle of that cover to entice the fish. Unfortunately, that means you are going to get snagged from time to time and loose some leaders and streamers. But, that's part of the game and if you want to catch crappie you have to pay for them by loosing a little gear.

There are two philosophies about dealing with snags. One is to go after the fly and try to unhook it from the object that has snagged the hook. That's good, sometimes you can retrieve your fly and avoid loosing it and some leader material. But, what if the fishing is really super, you're taking lots of good sized fish from that spot, and you know by tromping over to unhook or paddling into the weeds with your float tube, you will spook the fish and put an end to your afternoon's fishing? Do you tug until the leader breaks, reach as far down the leader as you can and cut it cleanly, or what? I guess it depends on how many fish you have, how much you are enjoying the fishing, and if you have another streamer you can use. The point is, you must think about the consequences of what you are doing before you make up your mind, and you should always carry enough spare leader material and extra streamers so an unretrievable snag won't suddenly end your fishing.

On the other hand, if you hook a fish and it tangles your line, you have to make a similar choice. You should always act in favor of retrieving the fish. You have, in my opinion, a responsibility to the fish and to yourself to retrieve it or allow it to escape while you are trying to retrieve it, rather than to cut the leader and leave it tethered to the weeds by the tangled line.

Smallmouth Bass Fishing

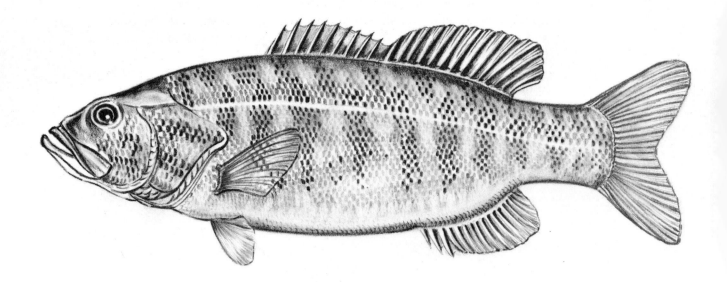

SMALLMOUTH BASS FISHING

To people not familiar with bass or bass fishing, an obvious question is: "What's the difference between largemouth and smallmouth fishing? Those fish are just the same except for the size of their mouths, aren't they?"

Actually, there is a good deal of difference between the two species and those differences have a great effect on how you fish for them and how successful your fishing will be.

It is amazing that two fish that are so closely related and look so much alike can really be so different. The smallmouth bass *(Micropterus dolomieui)* is, like its cousin the largemouth, a member of the sunfish family. It is a relatively slender fish and has a fairly large mouth, but its jaw does not extend past the rear edge of its eye. There is a shallow notch that separates the spinous portion of the dorsal fin from the soft rear portion. The smallmouth's back and sides are generally a greenish-brown color with subdued dark-colored mottling and several vertical bars. Its belly is usually a dirty shade of white.

Fishermen refer to the smallmouth by many names, like bronzeback, black bass, brown bass, and even green trout.

While the largemouth is usually found in still-water spots like ponds, lakes and reservoirs, the smallmouth prefers the clear, clean waters of moderately fast-flowing streams and rivers, though it does do well in some still-water impoundments.

Where they occur in ponds, lakes and reservoirs, smallmouths tend to concentrate near the mouths of rivers flowing into the impoundment, or in areas of the lake where current is created by the wind. When you are searching for smallmouths, the best place to start looking is that part of the lake where the water is the clearest and the cleanest.

In a stream or river, the fish congregate in spots with moderate current. They like to lie behind downed trees and behind rocks in small pools where there is a noticeable current, rather than in very slow-moving pools or those where the water is completely still.

Early morning solitude. Don Blegen photo

Smallmouths are usually associated with rocks in some form — gravel, boulders, scattered rock, or riprap. The fish need rock to spawn successfully and they prefer to spawn directly in the rocks, over gravel, or bottoms covered with sand. Biologists say smallmouth nests that are constructed in silty lake or stream bottoms are rarely successful.

Many anglers have misconceptions about smallmouth bass. Unfortunately, the smallmouth is a fish that prefers to live in cool, clear flowing waters rather than the warmer water normally found in reservoirs, lakes and ponds. Because they grow rather slowly and because many excellent smallmouth waters are in the north where the growing season is shorter than it is in the south, smallmouths just don't get as big as their largemouth cousins.

Because the smallmouth is not readily available in many parts of the country and because it is not capable of attaining real heavyweight status, it has not enjoyed the immense popularity of the more common largemouth.

On the other hand, the smallmouth can be more difficult to catch and it fights stubbornly until it either escapes, which is often, or is landed by the angler. One of its favorite tactics is to jump or roll on the surface trying to shake the lure from its mouth. If it can't throw the hook, it dives and heads for deeper water to continue the fight. In my opinion, smallmouths are the most acrobatic of all freshwater game fish. That's why I'd rather catch a 4-pound smallmouth on fly fishing gear than a 6-pound largemouth on the same equipment — smallmouths are just that much more exciting and fun to catch.

Smallmouths sometimes do well when stocked in lakes and reservoirs. They are best suited to those impoundments that have moderately clear water, some spots over 25 feet deep, and rocky points, reefs, ledges and other structure that supports a good population of crawdads (also known as crayfish in some parts of the country). Smallmouths tend to concentrate around river mouths and in areas where the wind produces some amount of current. Gravel pits sometimes produce good smallmouth fishing if they have good populations of crawdads and minnows present.

You must remember one thing above all else when smallmouth fishing with flies: most of your fishing will be done in sandy, rocky places, and that means the hook points on your flies are going to take a beating and will need frequent sharpening. Like the largemouth, the smallmouth has a tough mouth and bony jaw. A hook must be very sharp to penetrate that tough tissue, especially when you are trying to drive the point home with a limber fly rod.

To become a good smallmouth fisherman you must first train yourself to ignore, for a time, all of the information you've accumulated about fishing for largemouth bass. You have to adopt different tactics and force yourself to fish different types of structure.

Because smallmouths favor clear, moving water, they can usually be found at inlet areas where creeks flow into the lake, along rocky shorelines where wind keeps waves splashing against the shore, or in narrow channels between islands where the wind keeps water moving. When lake fishing, look for rocky points, small rocky ledges and shallow rocky or sandy reefs – spots where you'd expect to find crawdads. Once you locate crawdads, chances are you'll find smallmouth bass close-by. But crawdads aren't the only delicacies listed on the smallmouth's menu. They also have a fondness for water beetles, nymphs, leeches, grasshoppers, minnows and frogs. We use flies that imitate all of these critters for smallmouth fishing. In the spring I like to fish water beetle and nymph imitations around the inlet areas, casting up into the creek and letting the current wash the fly along, as it flows into the lake. This tactic also works well with grasshopper patterns from mid-summer into the fall because many fall into the water or are blown off the stream banks and are carried into the lake.

During the warm months I like to use leech flies and cast them around lily pads, cattails and masses of floating algae where live leeches are generally found. This is a case of casting as close to the vegetation as possible, and retrieving the fly while erratically making the leech swim with short darting movements. I try to retrieve the fly parallel to the vegetation to keep it in potentially productive water as long as possible on each cast. I spend a lot of time working small openings among the weed growth and fish them as carefully and thoroughly as possible with the leech.

The Deerhair Bumblepup Popper is an effective imitation of a small frog, another critter high on the smallmouth's list of favorite foods. To enjoy some exciting topwater smallmouth action, fish the popper about the same way you would for largemouth bass, except cast it to shallow rocky areas rather than to masses of shoreline vegetation. If the water is choppy and the waves are a little too large for effective popper fishing, try fishing beneath the surface with a Black and White Long Streamer. Use a sink-tip fly line to get the fly deep and give it the proper action to make it imitate a wounded minnow swimming around and over submerged rocks.

During the early spring, smallmouths cruise slowly along rocky dam faces or rock-strewn shorelines in both lakes and streams looking for groceries, and that means it's time to tie on a crawdad pattern. Cast the crawdad parallel to shore among or just off the rocks and make it crawl slowly back along the bottom. Give the line a sharp jerk occasionally to make the fly scoot a few inches and kick up a little silt from the bottom, like a live crawdad does as it scurrys away from danger.

When you're fishing crawdads in streams, try casting upstream and allow the fly to drift back downstream about like you would a nymph. Let the current carry the crawdad past you, feed out some line to continue the drift, and then retrieve it along the bottom in a series of short, darting jerks.

Always fish crawdad patterns near rocky areas in spots where you would expect to find real crawdads. I like to cast into shallow eddies where crawdads stay out of the direct current, but if I don't get a strike there I try to change my luck by casting into deeper pools.

Crawdad patterns can be dynamite when fished below dams in the tailrace area and in adjacent pools of slack water. If the river is shallow near the shoreline, try wading out and casting upstream parallel to the bank, so the current will carry your fly along the bottom in 4 to 6 feet of water.

We've found a good way to keep the fly down on or near the bottom is by using a weighted fly on a sink-tip line. When I must cast from shore I locate a spot where the current flows right along the shore, then let the fly move slowly down and past me, just like I would if I was wading.

The key to fishing a crawdad pattern in swift water is using enough weight to keep the fly moving slowly, instead of allowing it to be swept along at the same speed as the fast-moving current. When retrieving the fly across stream or upstream against the current, make it move in a series of very short darts and pauses along the bottom in the same manner a live crawdad moves.

Crawdads spend much of their lives in, around, and under rocks and ledges, and dense growths of aquatice vegetation. They are sensitive to light and like to hide in dark holes and shaded spots during the day. They do most of their foraging for food along shorelines at night, but on heavily overcast days they are sometimes active during daylight hours. You'll see them crawling slowly over rubble on the bottom with an awkward backward movement that causes them to fall or slide sideways off of rocks and other objects.

A crawdad sits on the bottom, usually near rocks or vegetation, waiting for food items to be washed to him. When disturbed, he scurries backward, and when threatened, he plants his tail and rears backward, raising his large pincers in front of him like a boxer to protect himself. When he retreats along the bottom his quick movements often stir-up bottom silt and you can follow his path by watching puffs of silt rise in the water.

Regardless of where they are found, smallmouth bass feed extensively on minnows because the small fish always seem to be in good supply in or near areas of vegetation, downed trees, fallen limbs, and shallow spots where bushes and trees hang out over and into the water.

One of our favorite minnow-imitating flies is the Black and White Long Streamer. It is very effective in various shallow-water spots where schools of minnows congregate. There is a tendency among fishermen to use streamers and bucktails that are too large. The adage big streamers for big fish may have some basis in fact, but we've caught plenty of large fish on small streamers. And, between hooking those large fish we've enjoyed catching many medium-sized fish that provided a lot of excitement.

We've had good luck in the spring with streamers and bucktails from 1½ to 2 inches long, which is about the size of live minnows most people normally use for crappie fishing. Later in the year, or in especially fast water, we use that same pattern tied a little larger, say 2½ to 3½ inches long.

I like to wade upstream when I'm streamer fishing. I try to concentrate on wading slowly while using natural cover to conceal my approach. Most of the smallmouths will be facing upstream into the current, and I think by quietly wading up from behind, I can get closer without frightening them, make better casts ahead of their position and control the fly as it moves back down to them.

Remember that minnows congregate in weed and grass beds where they can find forage organisms and hide from predators. Those are the areas you want to concentrate on when you are fishing streamers. Keep the fly close to the vegetation and retrieve it with movements that imitate a living minnow. Predators take injured or ill minnows first because they move slowly and are easy to catch, so try to make your fly imitate the erratic movements of a stricken minnow.

If you are going to be a consistently successful smallmouth fisherman, you have to learn to fish hellgrammite flies properly. Hellgrammites are the larval stage of the dobsonfly and many fishermen swear they are the bet bait you can use when stream fishing for smallmouths. Hellgrammites average 2½ to 3 inches long and range from brown to dark-brown to black in color. They have many legs on both sides of their slender bodies and seem to be flexible in all directions. They also have small, strong pincers that hurt if they nip you. They live under rocks and are most often found in stretches of stream where there are lots of riffles.

I always carry a few hellgrammite flies that have been tied with heavy bead-chain eyes because the extra weight lets me better fish the swift riffles where smallmouths lie in warm weather. Get off to the side of the current and cast the fly upstream and across, then let it dead-drift back. That allows the fly to sink into deep holes where the fish are used to finding large hellgrammites.

A common method for fishing smallmouth streams is to float the stream in a canoe until a likely-looking spot is found, then beach the canoe and fish the area thoroughly from shore or by wading in the river. When you have finished with that particular spot, the canoe is used to move to the next. It is easier to cover many miles of stream in this manner than to try to wade or walk the same distance.

I like to use a floating nymph in June and July and then again later in the fall when the fish might encounter seasonal emergences of what is known as the tiny western olive mayfly. Though this particular mayfly is most common in the West, the floating nymph has proven effective across the country for bass fishing. Maybe bass aren't as selective as trout, or maybe the nymph suggests another organism that bass like to eat, but whatever the reason, floating nymphs deserve a place in your smallmouth fly box.

This particular pattern actually is representative of the stage of the nymph that occurs just prior to its hatching into an adult insect. I like to cast it upstream and let it be carried downstream on or just below the surface when the current is moving near the stream bank.

One of my favorite dry flies to use for smallmouths is the Paradrake. It is a floating parachute-type dry fly that imitates the western green drake and other large mayflies. It has proven to be effective on ponds, lakes, reservoirs, creeks, streams and rivers, wherever cool, clear water is found near aquatic vegetation.

I like to cast the fly as close to standing vegetation as possible and let it sit several seconds before skating it a few inches across the surface. If that doesn't produce a strike, I recast to another location a few inches away. By casting and changing position often, I can work an area thoroughly and tempt every fish in the vicinity. I may not get them all to strike, but at least I'm confident they have seen the fly and been given the opportunity to hit it.

When I'm fishing the paradrake in a stream, I cast it upstream along the outside edge of a line of vegetation and let it ride the current downstream as close to the weeds as possible. This tactic works especially well in spots where the current is very slow. Sometimes it produces very swift, slashing, dramatic strikes; while other times a bronzeback will rise warily like a trout and just suck the fly from the surface.

In faster moving water I cast the fly upstream and try to place it so the current floats it around, past and behind submerged rocks or other obstructions where smallmouths are apt to be waiting for a snack to be served.

Largemouth Bass Fishing

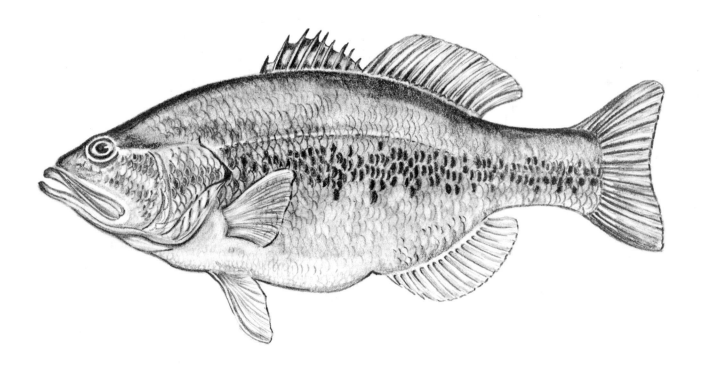

LARGEMOUTH BASS FISHING

The largemouth bass *(Micropterus salmoides)* is thought by many fishermen to be the greatest of all freshwater gamefish. Whether you share that opinion or not, there is no denying bass are fun to catch.

The largemouth is a slender, streamlined sunfish that is named for the size of its mouth. The upper jaw extends well past the position of the eye. The dorsal fin has two parts, a spinous portion and a soft portion that are separated by a deep, easily recognized notch. There is a broad, dark, continuous stripe that runs horizontally along its sides.

Largemouth bass vary in color depending largely on the quality of the water in which they live. If the water is dark and murky, the fish will tend to be pale, while those from clear water will have deep, rich colors. They are typically green to pale olive across the back, green on the sides with the distinctive dark lateral line, and pale white or yellow on the belly.

LARGEMOUTH BASS FISHING

The largemouth bass is one of America's most popular gamefish and has had a greater impact on sport fishing than any other single species. When bass fishing exploded into popularity a couple of decades ago, it set the stage for accelerated rod, reel, boat, motor and electronic fishing accessory development and created an atmosphere in which increased knowledge of fish and fishing techniques became important to even the average fisherman.

Fishermen pursue largemouth bass year-round, but most agree the best and most productive fishing occurs in the spring.

Bass fishermen usually equate their sport with stiff casting rods, heavy lines and large artificial lures, but regardless of how those fishermen view their world, fly fishermen have proven they can take the same number of fish and the same size fish as those using heavy equipment. In fact, in some instances the fly flinger may have an edge over other bass fishermen.

Fly fishermen have the opportunity of fishing a wide variety of fly types that imitate the sizes and types of critters bass eat at different times throughout the year. Because of limitations of their equipment, bass fishermen who restrict their fishing to spinning and bait casting gear are able to fish only lures that imitate a very few of the larger organisms bass consume.

The small size and light weight of flies and bass bugs necessary to imitate everything bass eat from nymphs to small fish, amphibians and crustaceans is of little consequence to the fly fisherman. He can cast his fly accurately and present it very quietly to avoid frightening wary fish. Fly fishermen have a definite disadvantage in only one aspect, namely, it's difficult for most flyrodders to fish very deep water. But, the good news is that a competent fly fisherman rarely needs to fish very deep to catch largemouth bass if he uses the right flies, fishes the right spots at the right times, and uses techniques and equipment suitable for the particular situation. Sounds simple, right?

Well, it can be, but it's also possible to do everything right and still come up empty. But hey! That's what it's all about. If a full fish basket was guaranteed every time you went fishing there wouldn't be much to hold your interest.

Largemouth bass fishing begins in the spring after warming temperatures melt all of the ice from the lake. Because farm ponds and other small bodies of water warm rapidly in the spring, bass fishing on these small waters starts earlier than it does on large lakes and reservoirs.

After a few warm spring days shallow water temperatures begin rising and largemouth bass drift into the shallows to feed. Many minnows and small fish look for food in that same shallow water and become food for the larger bass. Streamer and bucktail patterns are especially productive in the early spring because a bass is programmed to depend on minnows for most of his groceries, and a well-presented minnow-imitating fly is sure to attract his attention.

The fly fisherman should work "fishy-looking" spots as thoroughly as possible by making several casts before moving on. Because the fishes' metabolism is slowed by cold water, bass won't move very far for a bite to eat in the spring, nor will they expend much energy trying to capture a fast-moving lure. Fishing deliberately, thoroughly and very slowly will produce many more strikes than using a quick hit-and-miss, rapid retrieve system.

We recommend an 8-foot long fiberglass or graphite rod and size 7 or 8 weight-forward floating line for cold water bass fishing. Streamers such as the Black Ghost Bucktail, Woolly Bugger, and Super Silver Minnow, which were discussed in the section on crappie fishing, are excellent early season bass lures. We recommend sizes 1/0 to 8 for use on largemouths, though smaller ones will also take fish. Use a leader at least 7½ feet long, tapered to about 4 pounds at the tippet, and concentrate your efforts on fishing water from 1 to 5 feet deep.

Remember, bass are in the shallows feeding on small minnows which are there eating zooplankton and insects associated with vegetation growing in the warming water. If you can locate a shallow, weedy spot adjacent to a deep water dropoff, so much the better — bass will use the deep water travel lanes to move from one shallow spot to another.

Early season fly fishing requires accurate casting and deliberate, slow retrieves. Casts should be made from deeper water to shallow for several reasons. For instance, it allows the angler to fish the deep-water side of cover which is more likely to attract fish during certain parts of the year. It puts him in a position to guide a hooked fish away from weeds, branches and other obstructions. It also allows the fisherman to cast accurately to fish-holding shallow water spots that are difficult to see or recognize from the bank.

Heavy cover, like submergent and emergent weedbeds, weedy or brushy shorelines, and even logs, stumps and downed branches always attract early season bass. Sometimes fishermen accurately locate spots bass are using but fail to find fish because they don't work the area thoroughly. The best method is to start shallow — sometimes early season largemouths will venture into water less than a foot deep — and work slowly and methodically away from shore, covering every foot of potentially productive water along the way.

An angler fishing submergent weedbeds may have success using a wet tip or sinking tip fly line that puts the streamer low in the water where bass do much of their feeding.

Bass are usually considered to be rough-and-tumble fish, known for their hard strikes and stubborn fights when hooked, but several months of cold winter temperatures have a calming effect on even the largest, most belligerent old sow bass in the lake.

Linda and I fished a good-sized farm pond in late March a couple of years ago and that trip is a good example of how tentatively largemouth bass sometimes feed early in the year. Mild winters in Nebraska are about as rare as frost in the desert, but we'd struggled through a long mild winter that particular year. It hadn't even gotten cold enough to put more than an inch or so of crust ice on the lakes all winter, and no one had been able to do any ice fishing to speak of. We hoped that meant fly fishing would start a little earlier than normal, and, as it turned out, it did.

That particular day the air was chilly but the bright sunlight felt warm on our faces. The pond's water was fairly clear and there was a lot of brown, dead grass in the water along shore. It was too early for the vegetation to have started growing, the weather was still plenty cold, and deep-down we felt it was a little early for bass, but we were anxious to get away from the house and try our luck. There were some trees along the western bank at the north end, near the spot where a small shallow creek flowed very slowly into the pond.

I was still tying a No. 6 Super Silver Minnow to my leader when Linda started casting to a staggered line of shallow water stick-ups along the northern shoreline.

She laid her line along the inside edge of the line of stick-ups, across water no more than 2 feet deep and retrieved the No. 4 Black Ghost Marabou-wing Streamer very slowly. The streamer passed within inches of the stick-ups and she let it pause 8 - 10 seconds several times during the retrieve. Each time the fly paused, it sank very slowly in the water. It was a great technique and made the streamer appear to be very life-like, but she didn't get any strikes.

Casting for bluegill is a relaxing exercise.

She made three or four casts in the same spot without success, then tried the deep-water side of the stick-ups. Her first two casts produced no takers, but on the third cast the streamer suddenly stopped in the water. For a moment she thought it was hooked on a weed, but then she felt the fish move and she quickly set the hook. The ensuing fight was slow and Linda said it felt like she was trying to drag a small branch through the water. When she lifted the 2-pounder from the water, it was larger than she would have guessed as she fought it. "It didn't slam the fly like bass generally do, I'm used to pretty hard hits, but this cold water must have really slowed them down."

That's typical of cold water bass, sometimes they strike like trout take nymphs — they just gently suck in, shut their mouths and swim away. Don't expect hard strikes in cold water.

We hooked and landed nearly a dozen 2 to 3 pound bass on slow moving streamers that afternoon, and all of them came from fairly shallow water. I'm sure the fish were in the shallow water because it was a bit warmer than the deeper spots.

Shallow water can be the key to catching bass in early spring. Look for them in shallow areas of heavy cover near the bank. In addition to grass and weeds, good early season cover includes stumps, logs, rocks and brushpiles. Remember, though, wherever you fish, a slow retrieve is crucial for catching bass in cold water.

Largemouths eat about anything they can catch, including many species of baitfish, small gamefish, worms, leeches, frogs, crawdads, tadpoles, salamanders, grasshoppers, moths, the whole spectrum of flying insects, large nymphs, and occasionally small mice, muskrats, snakes, and even an occasional bird. In the early spring, minnows and small fish are among the most abundant forage available and are the easiest for sluggish bass to catch. Consequently, streamer and bucktail patterns are very productive choices for early season bass fishing.

Late winter bass fishing is usually an "iffy" proposition at best, but fly fishermen should be out fishing on those occasional nice early spring days, trying streamer patterns in shallow water around some type of cover. The angler may have a hot day and catch a lot of fish, or it may turn out that all he gets is a few hours of casting practice. But, whether he catches any fish or not, he'll find it's great to be out fly fishing after a long winter of doing chores around the house.

In some areas of the country, early April is considered to be one of the best times for bass fishing because the fish feed heavily while preparing to spawn. Spawning is controlled by water temperature, and water temperatures vary in different areas — it's best for the angler to get into the habit of using a water thermometer to determine when spawning is apt to occur where he fishes. Largemouth bass generally spawn when water temperatures are in the 62 to 65 degree range.

Before the spawn starts, when water temperatures climb over the 50 degree mark, bass begin moving into areas where they will later spawn. Throughout this period fly fishermen will find plenty of action in 1 to 3 feet of water near shore. The fish constantly prowl shorelines looking for food and are less selective in their feeding than at any other time of year.

We like to fish in the morning with Woolly Worms, Woolly Buggers, and Marabou Leeches in sizes 4 - 6, patterns that provide plenty of action to tempt the bass. By mid-afternoon when the sun is at its warmest, we switch to Deerhair Frogs or Bumblepups in sizes 2 - 6. This is the first legitimate opportunity of the year to fish floating bugs and enjoy the excitement of topwater strikes.

Try casting a Deerhair Frog near the bank where water is only a few inches deep and practice twitching the lure toward deeper water. Keep the rod tip pointed toward the frog and at about a 45-degree angle to the water so it will absorb the fish's energy when a strike occurs.

When the spawn is in progress it's the male's job to protect his nest, and he strikes viciously at just about anything that enters his area. Adult bass are easy to catch during the spawn, and because of heavy pressure on the nation's bass population, we recommend anglers allow the fish to spawn unmolested and that any bass taken be returned immediately to the water unharmed.

When the female bass finishes laying her eggs, she leaves the nest and moves to deeper water to rest and recover from the rigors of spawning. When the newly-hatched bass are able to fend for themselves they form schools, leave the nest, and head for shallow areas where they can hide and find food in the security of dense vegetation. When the fry leave there is no longer a need for the male to guard his nest, so he drifts off into deeper water and rests a few days before heading back into the shallows to feed.

Fishing improves after the fish rest a few days, and fly fishermen who spend as much time as possible on the water during this period, will be well rewarded for their efforts. Bass are very aggressive in the late spring and a variety of streamer and bucktail patterns as well as deerhair frogs and poppers will produce good action.

It is important to keep in mind that the largemouth is a predator that prefers to hide in or behind some type of cover so it can ambush its prey. The bass's body shape allows it to swim easily among weeds and other forms of cover and it is designed for short bursts of speed rather than fast swimming for long distances. Though it will occasionally chase potential food for a short distance, it is not a relentless pursuer like a northern pike or muskellunge. A bass would rather stick close to cover and strike quickly from ambush, wasting as little energy as possible while collecting its food.

Knowing that should have an effect on how a fly fisherman goes about trying to hook a bass. The most successful fisherman has learned to recognize and fish only cover where bass are apt to be hiding. He's learned to cast accurately and place his fly as close as possible to weeds, tree stumps, logs, and various other kinds of cover, trying to put the fly or lure right on the nose of a hiding bass.

The angler can increase his success during the hot summer months by fishing in the early morning, in the evening and at night when temperatures are coolest, and by intentionally avoiding the hottest part of the day which can be uncomfortable for both fish and fishermen. Bass search for food in shallow water while the water is cool, but when it warms they head for deeper, more comfortable areas out of the direct sunlight.

There's no time of day I enjoy being on the water more than in the early morning. The water is usually calm then, it's the coolest part of the day and so quiet I can hear what's going on all over the lake, and I like seeing all the things that happen around the lake early in the day. Many animals are still active at sunrise and while fishing I've seen a variety of wildlife species including: deer, coyotes, bobcats, moose, and antelope stop by for a quick drink before bedding down for the day.

All kinds of gamebirds and non-game birds are active in the morning. I enjoy listening to pheasants cackling while I'm pulling on my waders and seeing red-winged blackbirds flit from cattail to cattail while I'm wading to a promising spot, or hearing the rush of wings as teal zip past me while I'm casting. People who stay in bed late in the morning miss seeing and being a part of a whole separate special world that begins each day just at first light and lasts for only an hour or so.

I don't know if you have to get up early to enjoy good fishing, though some biologists say by the time most fishermen arrive at the lake, the majority of the fish have already moved back into deeper water. I do know if you arrive at the lake early, you'll enjoy the experience. There's a whole lot more to enjoy about fishing than just catching fish.

I remember how warm the water was as I sat in my float tube and kicked my way across tiny Wild Plum Lake early one mid-July morning. The sun was just climbing over the dam at the far end of the lake as I glided into casting range of a small cove littered with lily pads. I have mixed emotions about fishing lilies. On one hand, I love the pads in the summertime because they provide excellent fishing, but, on the other hand, I just hate to fish them because there are 1,000 ways for a fly or fly line to get hung-up.

It's best, especially for beginning fishermen, to shy away from fishing lily pad fields with streamers, bucktails or any other types of flies that are fished below the surface. I think lily pads are the most difficult and frustrating of all types of cover to fish with fly fishing gear.

Most fly fishermen fish lily pads by working the outside edge of the mass and that's not a bad idea. They use a streamer or other sub-surface fly to work the outside edge of the field, and that sometimes produces fish, but most of the bass stay within the mass, gliding through the maze of stems and roots in shade provided by the canopy of large round pads floating on the surface above them.

We've found that one of the best and most productive methods is to use high floating Deerhair Frogs or Bumblepups and cast them to small spots of open water within the lily pad field.

We cast among the pads and slowly pop our lures across the surface. We try to imitate the action of a small frog as it swims lazily on the surface, stops frequently to rest, then kicks forward a short distance before resting again.

Spots where shoreline vegetation emerges from the water are sure to produce bluegill and largemouth bass.

I tied a No. 6 dark green and white Bumblepup to my 4-pound leader and cast to a small spot of open water within the mass of bright olive pads. I popped the lure a couple of times and darn! I was hung-up already. My leader had cut through the top of a pad and the lure had become hooked underneath it on a stem. There was nothing to do but paddle into the mass of vegetation and loosen the lure.

Paddling a float tube into a mass of lily pads is like trying to leave a church service with a crying baby — there's just no way you can do it quietly and without causing a disturbance. But, I finally freed the fly and got my line untangled. I figured I'd spooked every fish out of the area, so I just sort of flipped the lure away, no more than 8 or 10 feet, so I could straighten my line and make another cast. When I flipped the Bumblepup away, it landed on top of a lily pad and laid there while I fiddled with my line. I had my rod tucked under my arm and was working with the line when the lure slid slowly off the pad into the water.

I've been startled several times in my life — I'll never get used to a covey of quail exploding from under my feet, and I know I'll always remember the time I almost stepped on the world's biggest bull snake while sneaking up on a small farm pond (someday I'll have to go back and get the tackle I threw all over the pasture that morning) — but what happened next ranks right up there with the worst of them.

The Bumblepup had drifted to within 6 or 7 feet of the float tube and I wasn't paying much attention to it. Suddenly the whole lake exploded! The only way I can describe the feeling is to have you imagine being all alone, floating on a calm lake on a quiet summer morning when someone in a helicopter overhead drops a cement block into the lake right next to your float tube. One second everything was peaceful, and the next, SPA-KLOOOSH!

Lily pads parted, water flew, my hat went one way, my sunglasses another, my heart took the express elevator right up the back of my throat, and I caught a glimpse of a large bass falling back into the water. I managed to grab the rod before it went clear under water, and when I picked it up, the line was whipping through the rod guides. I tried to set the hook but I was too late and I was almost impaled by the flying Deerhair Frog as it zipped past my head.

I don't know how big that bass was, but it doesn't matter. I'll remember the thrill that fish gave me at least as long as I'll remember the 5 and 6 pounders I've actually landed. In fact, not knowing how big the fish really was is more fun in a way, because I can imagine the fish and enjoy trying to guess its size over and over. That's what they mean when they say there's more to fishing than just catching fish.

That experience taught me that largemouths will take slow moving floating bass bugs. I've taken several good-sized bass since then by casting my lure onto a lily pad, waiting a few seconds, then pulling it gently into the water. Sometimes the strike comes immediately, sometimes only after I let the bug sit motionless in the water for a minute or more, and sometimes after I make it dart a few inches across the surface. The key is to try all of the tactics you can to tease that bass into striking. He's there, lurking below the lily pads, watching your lure. If you work it slowly and seductively enough he'll take it, and that's when the real fun begins.

Sometimes it gets so hot during the summer you just don't feel like battling the heat. That's when you should try fishing after dark. Moonlight bass bugging is a totally different experience, one every fly fisherman should enjoy at least once. Chances are, if you try it you'll be hooked on night fishing for good.

Everything looks different at night. The biggest difference I notice is that I loose some of my depth perception and it's more difficult for me to accurately place a cast when I can't clearly see the cover or background I'm casting to. The rules for night fish are about the same as during the day, except that everything must be more deliberate. You wade slower, more quietly, and try not to make any disturbance in the still night.

It is advisable to do your night fishing in areas you've become familiar with during the day. It is much more difficult to wade in an unfamiliar area at night than in one where you are sure there are no snags to trip over or holes to step into. But, regardless of how well you know the spot, it is a good idea to wear a life vest when fishing after dark.

Bass seem to become less wary and feed more aggressively at night, but they still prefer to stay close to cover rather than venture into large expanses of open water.

Floating Deerhair Bugs and Frogs are ideal for nighttime fishing. My choice of gear includes an 8½ to 9-foot rod rated for No. 8 or No. 9 floating line and a tapered 7½ foot long 6-pound test leader. I use dark colored flies one or two sizes larger than normal at night because I think dark, large flies are easier for fish to see silhouetted against the night sky.

I usually start by casting a dark-colored No. 4 Deerhair Frog as close as possible to shoreline vegetation. I try to make that imitation frog act like a real frog floating in the water. Real frogs sit motionless for long periods with only their eyes or heads above the surface, and when they move they dart forward a short distance underwater. When a frog swims it usually does so purposefully a few feet at a time, then floats back to the surface. Try to make your fly imitate those actions as closely as possible.

Most of my nightime strikes on deerhair frogs have occurred after the lure has floated motionless for several minutes and I've just started to make it swim forward. I start that movement with a short sharp Pop!, then make a series of quick, short jerks. If a bass is going to grab my lure it usually happens when I first pop the lure.

It is very important to keep the rod tip pointed at the frog and at an angle to the water, so when a strike occurs the force is absorbed by the rod rather than by the leader. The leader is apt to break or a knot to part if the force directed on it is great enough.

Keeping the rod at an angle also lets you set the hook quickly and keep the line tight so the fish is less likely to throw the hook.

I fish the shoreline thoroughly – and I mean thoroughly. I cast to every depression in the vegetation and any spots that even look like they might hold a fish. That means I move along the shoreline casting two or three times to about every 3 feet of shoreline, and if a particular spot looks especially attractive, I may make as many as a dozen casts there to cover every inch of the spot like a blanket.

I prefer to fish topwater Deerhair Bugs on cloudy, dark nights when the water is very calm. I fish only shallow water, about 4 feet deep or less, and I fish very slowly. I'm convinced one of the biggest problems fishermen have is that they fish too darn fast, whether fishing during the day or at night. For some reason the next spot you want to cast to always looks better than the one you're working on now, and it's hard not to hurry to get to it. But, if you want to catch more fish more often, you have to make yourself slow down. You have to control that urge to hurry and concentrate on fishing thoroughly and deliberately. Fishing is a relaxful, enjoyable activity – don't hurry through it.

If there are not many clouds and it is a fairly bright night, I prefer there to be a slight breeze which is just enough to put a slight chop, or really more of a ripple, on the water.

I always start bass fishing at night with a Deerhair Frog or Bumblepup. If the water's calm and I'm getting strikes I stick with it, but if the wind is blowing, the water is choppy and not much is happening, I'll use the bug for a while, then change to a sub-surface lure like a weighted Muddler, Marabou Muddler, or Sculpin Minnow. That's because I believe it is more difficult for the bass to see a floating bug when there is wave action on the lake and they are less likely to take a surface lure they can't readily see.

It is easy to control the depth at which you fish weighted Muddler and Sculpin patterns by varying the speed and type of retrieve.

The two best nighttime techniques for using sub-surface flies is to cast as close to cover as possible and vary the depth of the retrieve by using the countdown method until you locate fish. At night, bass can usually be found in the same spots you'd look for them on a spring day: near masses of lily pads, brushpiles, submerged weedbeds, partially submerged trees, logs and stumps.

A big bass likes to feed on big minnows. When he sees a No. 4 to 1 Muddler or Sculpin swimming near the surface or bouncing along the lake bottom, lights flash in his head, his mouth starts watering, his gills flare, and he attacks the fly like a kid after cotton candy.

Bass seem to be particularly aggressive when they feed at night and there won't be much question when a fish takes your Muddler. The strike won't have the same impact as a surface smash because the fish will probably grab the fly and head for cover in one pass, but you'll know he's on when the line goes tight and your rod whips into an arc.

As soon as you set the hook, start maneuvering the bass toward open water. He'll instinctively head for the security of dense cover the second he feels the hook and pull of the line. If you allow him to tangle your line or leader around any obstruction it is apt to break and you'll loose the fish.

After spending many nights on the water we've found a kind of routine or pattern to summertime night bass fishing. The fishing is usually good from about an hour before sundown until around 1 a.m., the action seems to slow down until about an hour before sunrise, when it picks up again and stays pretty good until the water warms about midmorning. Even though the action slows during the wee hours of the morning, you can still catch fish then and the action during that period is still far more productive than it is during the miserable midday hours.

But, night fishing really isn't for everyone, some people just can't fish at night or don't want to. One problem is mosquitos. Largemouth bass feed aggressively at night and so do those darn mosquitos. If there is a breeze they aren't much of a problem, but on a still night you can get chewed to pieces.

A mesh headnet and a light-weight long-sleeved shirt help a lot and good mosquito repellent is essential. But, you have to be very careful when using mosquito repellents because the good ones can damage the finish on your rod, reel and fly line. In addition to that, if you get any on the line, leader or fly, I'm sure it comes off in the water and it can't help but nauseate fish. Use a good repellent − the stronger, the better − but use it carefully and be sure it goes only on exposed skin. Wash your hands thoroughly after applying it.

If you are able to fish only during daylight hours, concentrate your efforts on the coolest parts of the day when bass are in easy-to-fish areas. When it gets hot and the sun shines directly on the water's surface, they head for shade and deeper, more comfortable water. Bass feed in deep water during that part of the day if they have a chance for an easy snack, and one of the easiest snacks they can encounter is a large minnow.

Verl Borg tying on a new fly.

When we use Muddler Minnows for summer bass fishing in water less than about 6 feet deep, we use weighted models rather than unweighted ones almost exclusively because we want them to sink rapidly. We feel we can keep them at the level we want to fish by using a floating fly line and using the correct retrieve.

There is a huge weedbed in a small cove on the west side of one of our favorite bass fishing lakes. The weeds are tall, emerging from the surface in 4-6 feet of water. Most of the bed is fishable with waders, but to get to the deep-water side, the side we want to fish when it's hot, we have to use float tubes or a boat. Our tubes usually get the nod at this particular spot because there are other spots nearby that we also like to fish that are difficult to work properly from a boat.

We paddle out to deep water a good distance away from the bed and move only as close as necessary to avoid spooking the fish.

I usually start fishing here with a weighted Muddler Minnow and Linda likes to use a weighted Marabou Muddler because she thinks the delicate action of marabou wing provides extra movement that entices hungry bass. She may be right.

The weedbed averages about 40 yards wide, so Linda starts fishing on one corner and I take the other. We cast parallel to the weeds on the deep-water side, as close to the weeds as we can, let the fly sink (stripping line off the reel as it sinks so it falls as vertically as possible), then start the retrieve.

I like to bounce the Muddler along the bottom, letting it drop into the soft mud occasionally. When that happens the fly disturbs the bottom and sends up a little poof of silt that can't help but draw the bass's attention. It tells him something is moving along the bottom, and chances are it's something that's good to eat. We catch a lot of big bass in the fall with this bottom bouncing technique. Try it at your favorite fall bass spots.

When it's hot you can sometimes have good luck fishing submerged weedbeds. If you can locate a weedbed in 4 to 8 feet of water, it may hold fish because it will be cooler, the water will contain a good amount of oxygen, and there will be small fish associated with the vegetation. Bass will be there feeding on the smaller fish.

I'm not a big fan of fly fishing deep water because I think shallow water fishing is both consistently more productive and a lot more fun. But, when we have to go deep to catch fish, we go deep. That involves putting the fly down deeper quicker, and that means using weighted flies and sinking lines.

The depth of the weedbed you want to fish dictates the type of fly line to be used. If the weedbed is fairly shallow, I like to use a wet-tip or floating/sinking line and try to swim my fly just above the tops of the weeds. If the bed is too deep, I use a sinking fly line to get the fly down deep quickly. In that case, I try to fish the edges of the weedbed to keep from getting snagged in the weeds. The one exception is if I use a Keel-hook streamer, in which the hook rides up and is less likely to snag than a fly tied on a conventional hook. If I'm using a Keel-hook streamer, I cast right into the weedbed and hope I don't get snagged.

I use the same techniques to fish submerged creek channels during the summer when fish can sometimes be found along the sides of the channel. I like to cast streamers parallel to the creek channel working up and down the sides of the channel with successive casts. If the spot is especially deep, I use both sinking fly lines and weighted flies to keep the fly as close to the bottom as possible.

If you are fishing shallow water with a rocky or gravel bottom in association with some type of aquatic vegetation, keep an eye out for crawdads scurrying along the bottom or among the rocks. If you see any, even just one, it's a good indication that others are around and you should try using one of your crawdad imitations.

Cast the fly near the weeds and let it sink to the bottom. Let it sit motionless for a period, then make it scurry along the bottom for a foot or so towards the rocks before letting it rest again. Then move it just a few inches a couple of times and let it rest again. If it stirs up the sand and gravel a bit as it moves, all the better. I even make my fly crawl up onto and over rocks to make it imitate the movements of a living crawdad. Crawdad imitating flies can be dynamite patterns when fished slowly in areas where bass are used to catching and feeding on large crawdads.

By the time September rolls around, Nebraska is usually up to its neck in grasshoppers. They seem to be all over the place, in people's lawns, gardens, in fields and pastures. Anywhere you find grass or weeds you're bound to find grasshoppers, and lots of them.

Many hoppers fall or are blown into creeks, streams, rivers, ponds, lakes and reservoirs, and anytime they hit the water they become fair game for hungry fish.

Even during the hottest times of the hottest days there are always a few bass that remain in shaded shallow areas, and it's those fish that feed most often on unlucky grasshoppers.

Cast your fly to spots where grasshoppers might actually be blown or fall into the water. Those spots include places where long grass and weeds grow along the bank, and locations where tree branches and bushes hang over the water.

When a real grasshopper lands on the water, it sits still for a few seconds, then struggles a bit trying to return to shore. Try to imitate those movements with your fly. Experiment with your line and rod to learn how to shake the rod tip to make the fly move a bit, how to strip short lengths of line to make the fly duck, dart, dive and swim. Learn to make the fly do exactly what you want it to, and you'll increase your ability to catch fish immensely. Just as with many other sports and worthwhile endeavors, the more effort you put into fly fishing, the greater your rewards will be.

Many fertile lakes and ponds experience enormous algae blooms that completely frustrate many fishermen. There are several types of algae and many of them can make fishing a real nightmare. The problem is simple — the algae clings to and coats line, leader and fly at every cast. There is no choice but to stop, wipe the green gunk off, and either try another spot or go home and mow the lawn.

Some forms of algae coat the surface with a greasy green slime, others suspend below the surface, and others seem to do both. Some algae that floats on the surface is pushed around the lake by the wind, so its location changes from time to time. Fish sometimes lie under the algae canopy shaded from the sun and fishermen can cast to edges of the mass and occasionally catch fish. All in all, algae isn't one of the best conditions for a fisheman to have to contend with. But, try your luck fishing when algae is present, maybe you'll work out a worthwhile system or technique that will allow you to catch some fish. Always try to find a solution to a fishing problem, it's part of the sport's appeal.

The fall fishing season begins when both daytime and nighttime temperatures start falling and the number of daylight hours decrease. Biologists say photo periods (or the number of daylight hours in the day) have more influence on all forms of wildlife than do weather or temperature changes. Whatever the cause, fish change their daily habits and movements with the seasons.

Wade slowly to thoroughly fish emergent shoreline vegetation.

The best way to understand fish movements in the fall is to think of it as a second spring. In the spring weather changes come quickly and often, but during the fall weather patterns are more stable and contribute to more consistent fishing action.

In the fall, largemouth bass again cruise shallow water during the day looking for food. There is a period of heavy fall feeding as fish acquire fat necessary to sustain them through the winter.

Because weedbeds provide many types of forage, bass spend a lot of their time searching them for food. Fly fishermen can use that tendency to their advantage by using streamers, bucktails and other minnow patterns to entice the feeding bass.

One difference between spring bass and fall bass is that a bass that survives the spring and summer is a smarter, more wary fish in the fall. Chances are he's seen hundreds of lures, has learned to rapidly seek cover when disturbed, and may have even been hooked and released a time or two. On the other hand, the angler should have developed his casting, fishing and wading skills during that same period. The fisherman must fish more deliberately and more delicately in the fall than in the spring to be successful.

Fishermen must be aware of what's going on with weedbeds in the fall. When the weeds begin to die and release carbon dioxide into the water, fish are apt to leave the area and move to spots where there is a larger amount of concentrated oxygen.

Later, after the weeds have been dead for awhile and are no longer releasing carbon dioxide, fish may return to them and fishermen might be able to catch them there again. Inlets bring fresh water and forage into the lake during the fall, just as in the spring, and fish will congregate at those spots again to feed. Look to the various forms of cover that produced fish in the spring, and work them slowly and thoroughly again in the fall.

It's strange that 45 - 55 degree days feel a whole lot warmer in the spring than in the fall, but the dedicated fisherman will stay on the water as long as the weather allows and learn to adjust his tactics to changes in the fishes' daily movements.

Hellgrammite Nymph

PART III

TYING THE FLIES

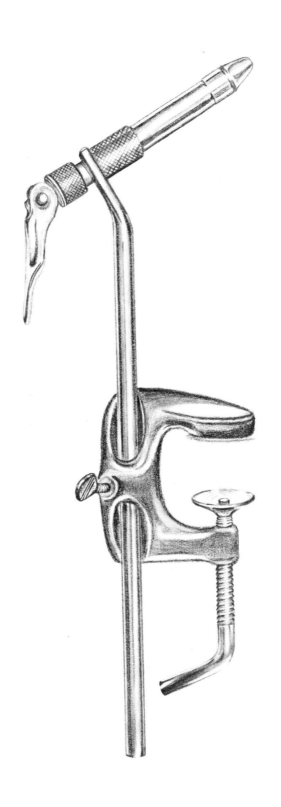

_____ FLY TYING EQUIPMENT

The tools a tyer uses are the basis for construction of a quality fly. Individual tyers have preferences for the types of equipment they use and we aren't about to say they're wrong. But, the tools we recommend for beginning tyers are well suited to do the job, are reasonably priced, and easily obtainable. There may be other brands and styles of tools that are just as good, or possibly superior to those we recommend, but these are the tools we use and suggest in our tying classes because we are familiar with them and know they'll do a good job.

FLY TYING VISE

The first, and probably most important tool a fly tyer will ever buy, is a fly tying vise. It's function is to hold the hook securely while a fly is being tied. We recommend the Thompson Model A vise, which has long been considered the standard against which most other vises are compared.

The Thompson Model A employs a single-action cam lever to hold and release the hook. The standard model has a clamp that secures the vise to a desk or table top, and the height of the vise is adjustable by moving it up or down through the body of the clamp. The jaws are adjustable to accommodate a wide variety of hook sizes and will hold them all securely. It sells for about $30.

An excellent addition to the Model A is a heavy pedestal base that holds the vise and allows it to be used without being clamped to the table top.

Unfortunately, most pedestal bases cost about as much as the vise itself, but if you intend to do a lot of tying you will find it to be a very handy, if not indispensable, accessory.

If your billfold is a little too thick around the first of the month, and you want to buy the vise we believe is the ultimate choice for the serious fly tyer, order the Regal Vise and accompanying pedestal. The jaws of the Regal Vise are operated by squeezing a handle lever on the side. When the lever is depressed the jaws are open; when it is released the jaws close tightly. Though Linda and I don't have one, we have used the Regal vise from time to time and recommend it highly if you can fit it into your budget. The vise is usually priced around $105; about $125 with pedestal.

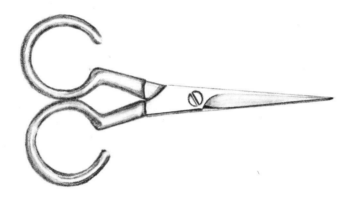

SCISSORS

Next to the vise, the tyer's most important tool is a good pair of scissors. In fact, we recommend you have two different types of scissors in reach while tying.

For most tying operations you'll need a scissor with very fine, sharp points. Tying scissors are similar to the small cuticle scissors women use to keep their fingernails in shape, but good tying scissors have even finer points and larger finger loops.

Fine, sharp points are necessary for getting into tiny places on a fly to trim threads and other materials. Large finger loops are important because you have to be able to pick the scissors up and use them quickly and easily. Many tyers like to keep the scissors dangling on their fingers throughout the entire tying procedure.

We like the Orvis scissors and the Skeeter scissors marketed by Wapsi Fly, Inc., of Mountain Home, Arkansas. A good pair of scissors costs between $5 and $10.

The second pair should be a heavier model for cutting coarser materials like hairs and furs, some heavy body materials, and even the thin lead wire used to weight flies. For the heavier scissors, we prefer the Fiskars brand, which is available in a couple of different sizes. Fiskars sell for about $3 to $10 depending on the size you want.

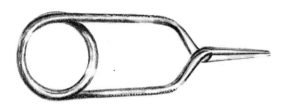

HACKLE PLIERS

We recommend you have three or four hackle pliers available when tying. Hackle pliers are your extra hands. They can be clipped onto the tip of a hackle feather to help you wind it, and they are invaluable for winding small hackle that is extremely difficult to grasp with your fingertips. They are also used to hold materials that are tied to the hook but aren't being used at the moment, and to keep the materials stationary until you need them.

We like Thompson hackle pliers because they are easy to handle and hold hackle and other materials well without damaging hackle quills. One side of the pliers' overlapping jaws is brass and the other has a grooved rubber pad. The pliers are made of flat strips of spring steel that do not twist in your fingers when you squeeze them together. A hackle plier costs around $3 from most suppliers.

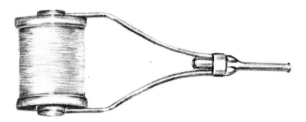

BOBBIN

The bobbin is made of spring wire that holds a spool of tying thread between its arms and has a hollow tube nose through which the thread passes. The bobbin keeps constant pressure on the tying thread by virtue of its weight, which means you can release the thread and use your fingers for other chores without being afraid materials you've already tied on the hook will come loose. The bobbin also allows you to wind thread easily and, because the tube is much smaller than your fingers, allows you to guide the thread in and around materials as you wrap and bind them to the hook. Bobbins are also used to hold and wrap spools of floss.

Linda and I tied for many years and produced thousands of flies without using a bobbin, but I have no idea why. Finally, we tried tying with a Matarelli bobbin and have continued using it for more than a dozen years. Now I think anyone who does not use a bobbin while tying is severely handicapping himself at the vise.

You can get by with one bobbin, but the more you tie the more you'll need additional bobbins and maybe a couple in different sizes. Be aware that the tip of the bobbin's tube may develop a rough spot or two after awhile, which can easily shred or break the tying thread. When you start breaking thread for no apparent reasn, check the tip of your bobbin's tue, it's probably time to get a new one. Bobbins usually cost around $6.

BODKIN

The bodkin is nothing more than a needle imbedded in a handle of some sort. It is used to pick out bits of dubbing material to give a fly a buggy look, to guide the tying thread or other materials into small places on the hook, to free hackle fibers that have been accidentally tied-down by the thread, and to do a variety of other things the tyer can't do with his large fingers.

Commercially manufactured bodkins are available for about $4.50, but we recommend making your own by merely forcing a long sewing needle through a cork of whatever size you choose. The homemade bodkin works fine and the cost is usually under a buck. Some people used discarded dental instruments as bodkins, but my aversion to pain and painful memories makes the needle/cork type a more attractive choice for me.

TWEEZERS

Every fly tyer should have a pair of tweezers in his arsenal for handling tiny materials. We prefer the type that is made of spring steel and is closed until you apply pressure to the arms to open the jaws. Tweezers may be purchased for $3 or so.

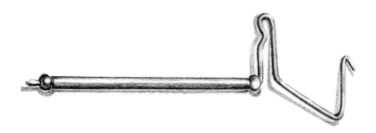

WHIP FINISH TOOL

A whip finish tool is used to make a neat, strong head on your fly. Many people use half-hitches for securing the head, but half-hitches can work loose after a few casts and loose thread lets the fly come apart. By performing the whip finish, the end of the tying thread is secured beneath several wraps of thread, and, after trimming, creates an attractive, strong head. I prefer to do the whip finish with my fingers, but Linda likes to use the whip finish tool because it helps her make excellent heads on tiny dry flies. Whether you use a tool or your fingers, you should finish your flies with a whip finish. Whip finish tools cost in the neighborhood of $6 to $7.

HAIR STACKER

A hair stacker is used to align the ends of deer, elk or moose hair before tying them onto the hook. Any small-diameter tube can be used, like the top of a lipstick tube, or an empty plastic film canister, and I've even used an empty shotgun shell with good results. But, commercial stackers work best because they pull apart in the middle so you can take the hair in your fingers easily after it is stacked. Hair stackers cost about $8.

MATERIAL HOLDERS

A material holder that attaches to the vise sleeve is a handy accessory to have when you are working with many types of materials at once. There are two basic types: one is a clip-model that hold materials between two parallel arms, and the other is a thin circular spring that just slides down over the sleeve. You just lay the materials between the spring wraps to keep them out of your way. Either type works well, and though not necessary, a material holder is handy to have around when you need it. You can buy one for $2 to $3.

LIGHT

You cannot tie a quality fly without a decent light. We prefer a swing-arm type lamp that can be easily adjusted to any position. They are available at discount stores in a wide range of styles and can usually be found on sale somewhere.

MISCELLANEOUS STUFF

Here are some suggestions for other things that might make your tying easier:

1. A sheet of white or tan poster board. We like to place a sheet of light colored, non-reflective poster board on the tying table behind the vise so the materials we're using and the fly being tied can easily be seen against the light-colored background. Sometimes materials, tools and tying instructions are laid on the table behind the vise and it becomes hard to see the fly while you're tying. Being able to see everything clearly helps your tying immensely.

2. Some people like to use a small pair of self-locking forceps as a combination tweezers-hackle plier, but we feel the tools designed for those particular jobs are better choices than the forceps.

3. There are many other tools available, including wing burners, hackle gauges, hackle guards, lances, waste baskets, etc., available from tying shops and mail order suppliers which are nice to have, but aren't necessary for the beginning tyer. These items, and a multitude of others, can be added as you need them.

WHERE TO BUY TOOLS AND MATERIALS

Unless you are lucky enough to have a fly shop or supply house near your home, chances are you are going to depend on mail order catalogues for most of your equipment and materials. Though I like to look at what I'm going to buy and hold it in my hands, that's not always possible and we've found mail order suppliers to be helpful and accommodating.

I think fly tyers should have a stack of current catalogues at hand when they are looking for a tool or type of material. That allows them to compare sizes, quality to some degree, and price. Get a current issue of a good fly fishing magazine like *Flyfishing, Fly Fisherman,* or *Rod and Reel* and obtain catalogues from their advertisers. Then you can enjoy looking at the catalogues, keep up on what's new, and do your shopping from the old comfortable Lazy-boy.

Here is a short list of some of the mail order suppliers we've done business with. I can't include them all, so I am including only the larger suppliers that have the most complete selections of tools and materials. There are also many, many small suppliers that do a fine job and I encourage you to do a little digging on your own and find a supplier that fits your needs. Some have smaller selections than others, some give a little faster service, and some are more personable than others – you just have to do a little shopping around. We've never had a bad experience with a mail order supplier, they have always been very helpful. Be specific when ordering, tell them exactly what tools you want and include their stock numbers. When ordering special materials we always enclose a sample of the size and color we need so the supplier can match it exactly.

Dan Bailey, P.O. Box 1019, Livingston, MT 59047; L.L. Bean Inc., Freeport, ME 04033; Kaufmann's Streamborn, P.O. Box 23032, Portland, OR 97223; Orvis, Manchester, VT 95254; Streamside Anglers, P.O. Box 2158, Missoula, MT 59806; Wapsi Fly, Inc., Rt. 5, Box 57E, Mountain Home, AR 72653.

TYING FLY PATTERNS FOR PANFISH AND BASS

The following patterns are our favorites for the particular species indicated, though some are effective for more than one species. For instance, one of my heaviest largemouth bass was caught on a Woolly Worm when I was fishing for bluegill, and I've caught several on crappie-sized minnow patterns. On the other hand, I've never caught a bluegill or crappie on a large Deerhair Frog or large Muddler or Sculpin Minnow.

The patterns listed are also chose to expose the beginning tier to a variety of tying techniques and different types of materials. We have modified some of the patterns a bit to make them easier for beginners to tie, and used materials that are easily obtained, inexpensive and easy for the beginner to use. We in no way claim that these are the standard methods for tying a pattern; that the pattern has to look exactly as ours does to be effective; that the materials we recommend must be used; or that the patterns have to be fished as we suggest to be effective. But we do know, without a doubt, that the patterns we present, tied as we explain, and fished in the manner indicated will catch fish. We are offering information accumulated during many years of teaching fly tying classes and fishing for panfish and bass in the hope of helping other fly tyers and fishermen.

We hope fly tyers and fishermen will use this information as a basis for further study and experimentation. Linda says she learns something new nearly each time she sits down to tie a few dozen flies. I know I learn a little on every fishing trip. Nobody knows all there is to know about either, and that's one of the things that make fly tying and fishing enjoyable.

WOOLLY WORM

Materials:
Thread: Black pre-waxed
Hook: Mustad 9672, sizes 8-12
Tail: Few strands red yarn
Body: Wide chenille (yellow,
  olive, black, brown, tan)
Hackle: One grizzly wet fly hackle
Lateral rib: Two strands peacock herl

The Woolly Worm is a very versatile pattern that will take many different fish species. It can be tied using several colors and color combinations, the most popular being yellow body/grizzly hackle, olive/grizzly, purple/grizzly, brown/grizzly, brown/brown, black/grizzly. Tie them both weighted and unweighted in sizes 1-12. In standing waters Woolly Worms are usually fished slowly with frequent pauses to allow the hackle fibers to vibrate and undulate in the water.

1. Secure hook in vise, attach thread and wrap hook shank with thread. Tie a small piece of red yarn at hook bend forming tail. Clip end of tail short, about even with widest portion of hook bend.

2. Tie in a grizzly hackle feather, two peacock herl and a 3- to 4-inch piece of chenille on top of hook in that order, at the same point where the tail was tied on. Tie grizzly hackle feather convex side towards the hook shank so when the feather is wound the hackle fibers will flare forward toward the hook eye.

3. Wrap tying thread forward, stopping 1/8-inch behind hook eye. Wind chenille forward forming body, and tie off behind hook eye where thread wraps ended. Trim excess material.

4. Pull peacock herl forward over top of fly creating the lateral stripe, and tie off behind hook eye. Trim.

5. Wind grizzly hackle forward Palmer style around the hook shank and through the chenille body. Tie off behind hook eye and trim.

6. Form head, whip finish, trim and cement.

LIGHTNING BUG WET FLIES

Materials:
Thread: Black, pre-waxed
Hook: Mustad 3906B, sizes 10-12
Tail: Black goose biot
Abdomen: Pink, orange or yellow
  flourescent yarn or chenille,
  also silver sparkle chenille
  can be used
Thorax: Small black chenille
Hackle: Black hackle feather

Lightning Bug Wet Flies are fairly simple to tie and are very effective for bluegill. We think the best way to fish them is along weedbed edges, a line of stick-ups or other form of shallow-water cover. In most cases we use non-weighted models, but we always carry a few weighted flies in case we want to fish a little deeper in the water. A slow, steady retrieve with frequent quick, short jerks is hard to beat for attracting hungry bluegill.

1. Secure hook in vise and tie thread to hook shank. Tie black goose biot fiber onto hook shank above barb to form tail.

2. Tie in a short piece of fluorescent yarn or chenille at the point where tail is tied on. Wrap material forward about one-half way down hook shank. Tie off material and trim.

116

3. Tie in a short piece of small black chenille just ahead of the abdomen material.

4. Wind the small black chenille forward forming thorax. Stop wraps just behind hook eye. Tie off chenille and trim.

5. Tie in a black hackle feather with concave side of feather towards the hook shank, so fibers flare back towards hook bend when wound.

6. Make two or three turns of hackle around hook shank, tie off and trim. Wrap thread back over hackle fiber bases just enough to make them flare backward over thorax. Form head, whip finish, trim and cement.

GIRDLE BUG

Materials:
Thread: Black, pre-waxed
Hook: Mustad 9672, sizes 10-12
Body: Medium-sized chenille, color optional
Tail: Rubber legging material
Legs: Rubber legging material
Weight: Fine lead wire

The Girdle Bug is a favorite bluegill pattern because it is very effective and is easy to fish. It is usually tied unweighted so it floats while the tiny rubber legs shimmy on the water's surface. (We weighted this pattern in the instruction because there are times when you want the fly to sink to the bottom rapidly. Tying the unweighted model is just the same, except you eliminate wrapping the hook shank with lead.) We like to cast girdle bugs into shallow grassy areas and fish them very slowly. Let the bug sit on the water for 30 seconds or more, then twitch the rod tip to make it move a few inches. Then let it sit several seconds before moving it again. This pattern works best on clear, warm days when the water is calm. We do occasionally fish weighted girdle bugs when it's hot and the fish are somewhat deeper. A good method then is to cast near vegetation, let the bug sink and retrieve it slowly with occasional darting movements, which make the rubber legs bend back along the bug's body, then flare out again as it sits motionless on the water.

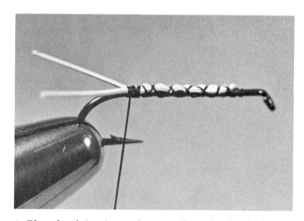

1. Place hook in vise and secure thread to hook shank. Tie two short pieces of rubber legging material along top of hook shank and wrap thread around the bases of the rubber material and between rubber pieces to secure, forming a forked tail.

2. Tie in a 6-inch length of black chenille at point above hook barb.

118

3. Make two or three wraps of black chenille around hook shank and secure with a wrap or two of thread.

4. Lay a 3-inch piece of rubber legging material across hook shank just ahead of the chenille and secure to the hook by figure-8-ing the thread. Legs should extend straight out from hook shank at 90 degree angles. Wrap lead wire around the hook shank from the point where the legs are tied to a point about 1/8 inch behind hook eye and secure with tying thread.

5. Make two more wraps of chenille ahead of legs and secure with thread.

6. Tie in a second set of legs and secure to hook shank by figure-8-ing the tying thread as before.

7. Make a final single wrap of chenille ahead of the second set of legs and tie off just behind hook eye. Form head, whip finish, trim, and cement. Trim legs as shown.

SPONGE-BODIED BUG

Materials:
Thread: Black, pre-waxed
Hook: Mustad 9672, sizes 10-12
Tail: None
Body: Sponge rubber body in green,
*   white, creme or black*
Legs: Rubber legging material
Hackle: None
** Most sponge rubber bug bodies are made for size 8 hooks. When tying for bluegill it is necessary to trim the body a bit to make it fit the size 10 or 12 hooks you'll be using.

Many fishermen think using a Sponge-bodied Bug is the only way to catch bluegill. It is easy to see on the water, it floats like the proverbial cork, and bluegill love it. What more could you ask? We use it in stained water because we think its bulky body is easier for the fish to see than the slimmer girdle bug under those conditions; and cast to the same spots where we use a girdle bug in clear water.

1. Tie thread onto hook shank above the barb and wind it to the hook eye and back again, then forward to a point about 1/3 way down the hook shank. Select a sponge rubber body and trim it to fit the hook as shown. Cut a shallow slit in the bottom of the body so it will fit around the hook shank. Coat thread windings along rear 1/3 of the hook shank with cement and set body on hook with shank pushed up into the slit. Allow cement to dry.

2. Wind thread around sponge rubber body and hook shank two or three times to secure the body. Pull body away from hook a little to allow thread to be wound forward on hook shank under the body another 1/3 of the way along the hook shank.

120

3. Apply head cement between spot where body is tied to hook and where thread is now located. Press body down along hook shank in that area, and wind thread around body again. Wind thread forward to point just behind hook eye. Secure front portion of the sponge body just behind hook eye, form head, whip finish and cement.

4. Thread strand of rubber legging material through eye of a sewing needle and, using needle pull strand through middle part of body as shown.

5. Add another strand of rubber legging material as shown in photograph. Trim to about 1 1/2 times length of the hook shank.

GOLD-RIBBED HARE'S EAR NYMPH

Materials:
Thread: Brown, pre-waxed
Hook: Mustad 3906, sizes 10-16
Tail: Hairs from hare's mask or ears
Rib: Gold wire
Body: Hare's ear dubbing, in various
*   shades of gray or brown*
Wingcase: Brown turkey quill fibers
Weight: Small diameter lead wire

The GR Hare's Ear Nymph is a good all-around nymph pattern that will take a variety of fish species under many conditions. We carry several in different shades of brown, gray, and olive, and a half-dozen all-black ones. We fish them near vegetation on or very near the bottom. In standing water we retrieve them slowly and a bit erratically across the bottom, allowing them to swim off the bottom a few inches for short distances. In the spring we cast into water flowing into the lake or pond and let the current wash the nymph along. Fish usually pick nymphs up gently, which sometimes makes it difficult to detect a strike. The angler must watch his line carefully and set the hook whenever it appears something out of the ordinary has happened to the fly. If the line stops, speeds up, goes slack, tightens, or twitches differently than normal, it may be an indication a fish has taken your nymph. Set the hook, if you're wrong you haven't lost anything, if you hesitate you may loose a legitimate strike.

1. Secure hook in vise and tie thread to hook shank. Tie a small bunch of hair from a hare's mask or ears onto the hook shank above the barb to form a short, semi-bulky tail. Tie a 4-inch piece of gold wire in at the point where the tail was tied on.

2. Weight front portion of hook shank with lead wire and wrap thread around and through wire wraps to help secure it to hook, then return thread to point on shank where tail is secured. Cover lead wire wraps with cement.

3. Spin dubbing material on tying thread in normal manner and wrap forward just a little over one-half way down hook shank forming a tapered abdomen. domen.

4. Wrap gold wire forward in even turns ribbing fly. Tie wire off and trim.

5. Coat a section of turkey quill with cement and let dry. Cut a 1/8-1/4 inch wide section of cemented turkey feather fibers from quill, and tie in just ahead of the abdomen with fibers extending back towards hook bend.

6. Spin more dubbing onto thread and wind forward forming thorax, making this section bulkier than the abdomen. Wrap to a point just behind hook eye.

7. Pull turkey quill section over the top of the dubbed thorax and tie down forming wingcase.

8. Trim excess turkey fibers, form head, whip finish, trim and cement. Use the point of your bodkin to tease fibers away from the dubbed thorax making it look very scruffy.

BLACK BIVISIBLE DRY FLY

Materials:
Thread: Black, pre-waxed
Hook: Mustad 94840, sizes 10-14
Tail: Black hackle fibers
Body: Black dry fly hackle
Hackle: White dry fly hackle

The Black Bivisible Dry Fly is an excellent multi-purpose panfish pattern that imitates a number of small flying insects. It floats well and has the advantage of being easy to see due to the white hackle at the front of the fly. It is usually most effective when fished near grasses and other forms of vegetation where insects are normally found. Tie this pattern in a variety of sizes and use during calm evenings when there are many insects on the water.

1. Secure hook in vise and attach thread to hook shank above barb. Place a small bunch of black hackle fibers on the hook shank above barb and secure with thread to form tail.

2. Tie in two black dry fly hackle feathers by the butts at the point where tail was secured. Tie them with the convex side parallel to the hook shank. Advance thread to a point about 1/16 inch behind the hook eye.

3. Wind the hackle feathers up the hook shank toward the hook eye in closely placed wraps to form as thick a hackle fiber body as possible. Tie off with thread and trim excess hackle.

4. Tie one white dry fly hackle feather in just ahead of the black hackle body, convex side parallel to hook shank, and wind thread forward to a point just behind hook eye.

5. Make two or three turns of white hackle around the hook shank and tie off with thread. Form fly head, whip finish, trim and cement.

LETORT CRICKET

Materials:
Thread: Black, pre-waxed
Hook: Mustad 9672, sizes 10-14
Body: Black dubbing
Underwing: Black duck pointer quill fibers
Overwing: Black deer hair
Head: Black deer hair

The Letort Cricket is an excellent late summer and early fall bluegill pattern. It is tied to imitate a cricket that has fallen or been blown into the water from along the bank. The most effective fishing method is to cast a cricket along the bank where grass, weeds or other types of vegetation hangout over the water. Fish get used to feeding on terrestrials in these spots and take an imitation without a lot of close scrutiny. Sometimes bluegill-sized grasshopper patterns discussed in the bass fly sections produce well in these same spots.

1. Attach thread to middle of hook and wrap backward to point above hook barb. Spin black dubbing material onto thread.

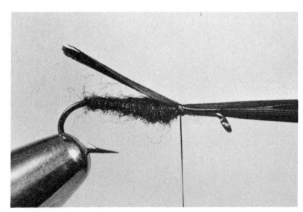

2. Wind dubbed thread forward about 2/3 of way up the hook shank forming a tapered body, thinner at the tail and thicker toward the eye.

3. Cut a section of black pointer quill about 3/8 inch wide from feather. Fold in half length-wise and apply head cement to both sides. Lay the wing along the top of the hook shank so it extends back even with hook bend. Attach wing to hook shank with thread immediately ahead of the dubbed body. Trim excess feather away.

4. Spin black deer hair in the normal manner to form fly head. Pack deer hair very tightly and tie-off behind hook eye. Whip-finish and cement to secure thread.

5. Remove fly from vise and trim as illustrated, leaving some deer hair fibers at rear of head to sweep back over fly body.

IMPROVED MCGINTY WET FLY

Materials:
Thread: Black, pre-waxed
Hook: Mustad 3906, sizes 10-14
Tail: Red hackle fibers
Body: Small black and yellow chenille
Hackle: Yellow hackle feather

Every fly fisherman has a favorite pattern, and I have to admit to being partial to the Improved McGinty Wet Fly for bluegill fishing. I usually start fishing with an Improved McGinty because I have great confidence in it. I really think that under most conditions I can quickly locate bluegill with it, and, I figure if they won't take a McGinty, "they ain't gonna take nothin!" I'm really not sure why the pattern is so effective − it looks like a bee, and maybe bluegill like bees, but it might be the flash of yellow and red they see in the water that triggers a strike, rather than the fly actually imitating anything specific. At any rate, bluegill love this fly and I use it a great deal. I'm sure you'll find it effective, too. Tie it both weighted and unweighted in sizes 10, 12, and 14. I sometimes think using this fly gives you an unfair advantage over the fish − it's that good!

1. Secure hook in vise and tie thread onto the hook shank. Tie a small bunch of red hackle fibers above hook barb to form tail.

2. Tie a 3 inch length of yellow chenille and a 3 to 6 inch length of black chenille at point above hook barb.

3. Pull black chenille parallel to hook shank and make two wraps of yellow chenille around hook shank and black chenille. Secure wraps with tying thread.

4. Pull yellow chenille parallel to hook shank and make two wraps of black chenille around hook shank and yellow chenille. Secure with tying thread and trim excess black chenille.

5. Make one more wrap with yellow chenille, tie off and trim.

6. Tie a yellow hackle feather in by the butt, concave side facing hook shank.

7. Wrap hackle two or three times around hook and wind thread back over hackle fibers to make them flair backward over body. Tie hackle off and trim. Form head, whip-finish, trim and cement.

BLACK GNAT WET FLY

Materials:
Thread: Black, pre-waxed
Hook: Mustad 3906, sizes 10-14
Tail: Black hackle fibers
Body: Small black chenille
Wings: White pointer quill slips
Hackle: Black hackle feather

The Black Gnat is a traditional pattern that has proven it's effectiveness in producing trout through the years. It is also one of the best bluegill flies you can use. It can be tied as a dry or wet fly, but we prefer it as a wet fly. It can be tied with a wing or without, but we prefer it without because it is easier and quicker to tie and the wing does not seem to make any difference in its effectiveness for bluegill, I don't know if that is true of trout. We fish it much the same as the improved McGinty and it seems to be especially effective in stained water where it can be seen easier by the fish than lighter-colored fly patterns.

1. Place hook in vise and secure thread on hook shank. Tie a small bunch of black hackle fibers above hook barb to form tail.

2. Tie in a 3 inch length of black chenille above hook barb, advance thread to the hook eye. Wind chenille forward around hook shank to a point just behind hook eye. Tie off and trim.

130

3. Tie a black hackle feather in by the butt, concave side towards hook shank.

4. Wrap hackle two or three turns around hook shank, tie off and trim. Wind thread back over hackle fibers to make them flair back over body. Form head, whip finish, trim and cement.

** Described above is the quickest, easiest method of making the Black Gnat, though the traditional pattern calls for the addition of a pair of white wings. To tie that pattern follow the steps above, with the exception of stopping the body just a bit further behind the hook eye, and add the following:

5. Cut identical slips from opposite pointer quills, marry the slips and tie them in just ahead of hackle to form wings laying over fly body.

6. Tie off securely and trim ends that extend over hook eye. Form head, whip finish, trim and cement.

McGINTY DRY FLY

Materials:
Thread: Black, pre-waxed
Hook: Mustad 94840, sizes 10-14
Tail: Red hackle fibers
Body: Black & yellow small chenille
Wings: White-tipped mallard wing feathers
Hackle: Brown dry fly hackle

In my opinion, using dry flies for bluegill fishing is unnecessary — you don't have to do it to catch fish — I can't think of any times when wet flies won't work just as well. But, dries are a lot of fun to use and that's why we fish — to have a good time. There is a lot to be said for seeing a fish take a fly from the surface, especially if it's a fly that was born in your vise. And, when it comes to taking surface-feeding bluegill, the McGinty Dry Fly is a very effective pattern. Some anglers like to coat their flies with floatant because after a fly has taken several fish, or has been cast several times, it can become water-logged and have a hard time floating. If you want to use fly floatant that's fine, but we just make three or four false casts to dry the fly.

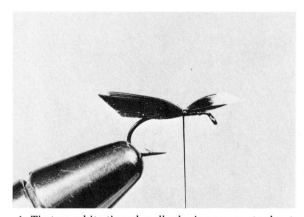

1. Tie two white-tipped mallard wing segments about 1/3 way down the hook shank behind the hook eye. Tie the segments in with their tips extending out over the hook eye.

2. Pull wings straight up, perpendicular to the hook shank and take several turns of thread in front of wings to make them stand.

132

3. Wind thread backward along the shank to the hook bend and tie in a small bunch of red hackle fibers above the hook barb to form a tail. Tie in a 2 inch length of small black chenille at point where the tail is secured.

4. Make two turns of black chenille around the hook shank and attach a hackle plier to the end to keep tension on it. Tie in a 2-inch length of small yellow chenille and advance thread forward by making a few wraps around the hook shank. Pull the black chenille forward, parallel to the hook shank and make two wraps of yellow chenille around the hook shank and the black chenille.

5. Tie the yellow chenille off with the thread and wind thread forward. Pull yellow chenille forward parallel to hook shank and make two wraps of black chenille around hook shank and yellow chenille. Secure both pieces of chenille with thread and trim excess chenille away. Tie two brown dry fly hackle feathers in behind the wings, convex side parallel to the hook shank.

6. Winding the hackle feathers one at a time, make two or three turns behind the wings, then two or three turns in front of the wings. Tie the feathers off and trim the excess. Form head, whip-finish, trim and cement.

ADAMS IRRESISTIBLE

Materials:
Thread: Black, pre-waxed
Hook: Mustad 94840, sizes 10-12
Tail: Dark moose fibers
Body: Gray or tan deer or caribou hair
Wings: Grizzly hackle tips
Hackle: Two grizzly, one brown
*   dry fly hackles, mixed*

The Adams Irresistible is another fly that made its fame as a trout slayer, but is also very effective for bluegill. Deer and carabou hair are both light weight and hollow, and when spun properly on a hook produce a fly that floats high and long. It can be tied with natural-colored as well as dyed hair. We usually use natural-colored or black Adams Irresistibles, but you may want to try any number of colors to see what works well in your part of the world. This pattern is especially effective in the evening when the water is calm.

1. Tie a small bunch of dark moose hairs on top of the hook shank forming a tail about as long as the hook shank. Secure the windings with a drop of head cement.

2. Cut a bunch of deer or caribou hair about one-half the diameter of a lead pencil from hide. Trim both ends of the hair and lay it along top of the hook shank. Make two wraps of thread around the hair and pull it tight causing the hair to flair. Allow the hair to flair and spin around the hook shank on its own.

3. Make another wrap of thread and pull tight, then advance the thread to a point directly in front of the spun hair. Tie in several more bunches of hair and compress each bunch of flared hair against the last as tightly as possible to create a compact fly body. Body should extend only one-half the length of the hook shank. Tie off to secure deer hair.

4. Remove fly from vise and trim body to a tiny cone shape with scissors as illustrated.

5. Replace hook in vise and re-tie thread to hook shank just ahead of fly body. Choose two grizzly dry fly hackle tips and match them for length and width. Lay them on top of the hook shank with tips extending out over the hook eye.

6. Secure them with a few thread wraps and then pull them up perpendicular to the hook shank and make a few thread wraps in front for support to make them stand. Separate the wings with your fingers and trim excess feather.

7. Choose one brown and two grizzly dry fly hackle feathers and trim them to identical lengths. Tie hackles in behind the fly wings and wrap hackles one at a time behind and in front of the wings. Make an equal number of wraps behind and in front of the wings.

8. Try to wrap them straight up and down to better support the fly's weight. Leave enough room to tie a head behind hook eye. Form head, whip-finish and add a drop of head cement.

DEERHAIR POPPER

Materials:
Thread: Black, pre-waxed
Hook: Mustad 3906B, or Mustad 1043
   Stinger, sizes 8-12
Tail: Deer hair, color to match body
Body: Deer body hair, color optional
Legs: Rubber legging material

The Deerhair Popper floats under even the harshest conditions, though it is most effective in calm water where the fish can easily see it. It is very effective when made to imitate a miniature live frog. We let it sit on the water for several seconds, then make it jump and twitch in the water with fairly long pauses between movements. It is most effective in the evening and morning when fish are feeding in shallow water. Cast close to cover and watch the fly closely. Set the hook as soon as a strike occurs.

1. Secure hook in vise and attach thread to hook shank. Tie in a few deer hair fibers forming a tail.

2. Cut a small bunch of deer hair from the skin patch. Pull out small hairs and fibers and trim tips. Spin deer hair about 1/3 of the way down the hook shank toward the hook eye. Tie on rubber legging material just in front of the spun deer hair and figure-8 the thread to secure legging material to hook.

3. Continue spinning deer hair another 1/3 of the way toward the hook eye, and secure another piece of legging material just ahead of this bunch of deer hair.

4. Spin more hair on the hook shank to a point just behind hook eye. Form head, whip finish and cement.

5. Remove hook from vise and trim deer hair as shown. Be very careful so you don't accidentally cut the legging material. Trim the deer hair on the bottom of the popper as close to the hook shank as possible so there is a good amount of space between the point of the hook and the bottom of the popper. That distance has to be as wide as possible to improve the chances of successfully hooking a fish.

SUPER SILVER MINNOW

Materials:
Thread: Black, pre-waxed
Hook: Mustad 9672 or 9674, sizes 4-10
Tail: Mallard breast or flank feather fibers
Weight: Lead wire
Underbody: Silk floss
Body: Flat silver tinsel wrapped to cover floss
Wing: Blue, yellow, white, orange and
  light green marabou
Overwing: Mallard breast or flank feather

The Super Silver Minnow is an excellent minnow-imitating fly. Tie it in a number of sizes and always have a few with you in your fly box. We also tie this pattern with mallard breast feathers that have been dyed green, gold, or black. Sometimes in different parts of the country or in waters that are stained to various degrees, one color will-outproduce others.

When we fish this pattern we try to make it imitate a crippled or wounded minnow as closely as possible. Predator species are attracted to crippled prey because it is easier for them to catch. We recommend a slow erratic retrieve close to crappie holding cover, like partially-submerged trees and weed beds. Try retrieving it at various depths until you find fish. The Super Silver Minnow is not only a deadly crappie pattern, it will also take largemouth and smallmouth bass, walleye, northern pike and other species when tied in appropriate sizes.

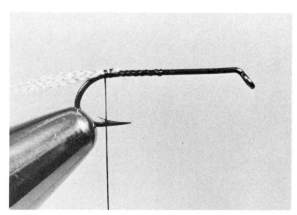

1. Place hook in vise and secure tying thread to hook shank. Tie in a small bunch of mallard flank or breast feather fibers at bend of hook for tail.

2. Wrap front third of hook shank with lead wire, wrap tying thread through wire and cement.

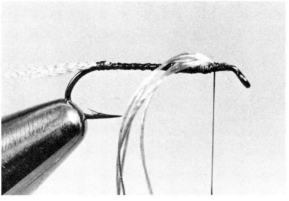

3. Tie in a 6-inch length of silk floss (any color) just ahead of the lead wire.

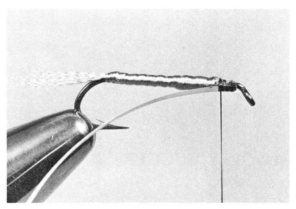

4. Wrap floss backward to point where tail was tied on. Wrap the floss forward again, forming a smooth body. Tie in a 6-inch length of flat silver tinsel behind hook eye.

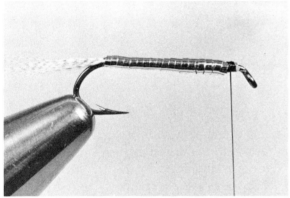

5. Wrap tinsel backward completely covering floss body, then wrap forward again. Tie off behind hook eye and trim excess tinsel.

6. Tie in a small bunch of white marabou feather fibers about 1/4 inch behind hook eye.

7. Repeat with each successive color of marabou and then trim tips so none of the fibers extend over hook eye.

8. Select a mallard flank or breast feather that is about half-again as long as the hook shank, and has a fairly straight stem. There should be an equal amount of feather fibers (barbules) on each side of the stem. Tie feather in along top of hook shank with concave side down along the shank, so the feather bends downward beyond the hook bend. Form head, whip finish, trim and cement.

WOOLLY BUGGER

Materials:
Thread: Black, pre-waxed
Hook: Mustad 9672, sizes 6-12
Tail: Black marabou
Body: Black chenille
Hackle: Black hackle
Weight: Lead wire

The Woolly Bugger has recently burst upon the fly fishing scene as a kind of super fly. It is very easy to tie, has excellent action in the water, and is attractive to a number of fish, including large crappie. The more erratic the retrieve, the more movement is imparted to the fly. I'm not sure what fish think it is — some experts say it imitates a leech, others say a minnow, and still others say a small snake, worm or large nymph of some sort, or a number of other critters. But, what it imitates really isn't important. Fish love it! That's the important thing. They love green, brown, black, yellow, white, red, and purple Woolly Buggers, and combinations of some of those colors. Tie them in a variety of sizes, both weighted and unweighted, keep a few handy, and use them often. Fish them near and over different types of cover at various depths and vary the speed of your retrieve until you find fish, then stick with whatever is working and have a good time!

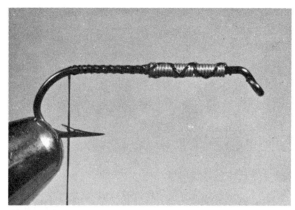

1. Place hook in vise, secure thread to hook shank. Wind lead around front half of hook shank. Wrap thread over and through wire wraps and cement to secure.

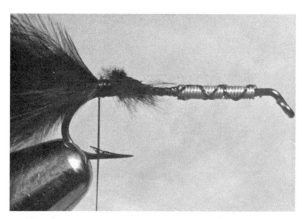

2. Wind thread back along hook shank to point above hook barb. Tie in a clump of marabou feather fibers. The fibers should be at least as long as the hook shank.

3. Tie in a black hackle feather, convex side toward the hook, and then tie in a 6-inch length of black chenille, wind thread forward to a point about 1/8 inch behind hook eye.

4. Wind chenille forward forming long, slender body. Tie off with thread and trim.

5. Wind hackle feather forward in even wraps. Tie off behind hook eye and trim.

6. Form head, whip finish, trim and cement. This pattern is basically a Woolly Worm with a long, thick, flimsy tail.

MICKEY FINN STREAMER

Materials:
Thread: Black, pre-waxed
Hook: Mustad 9672, sizes 6-12
Body: Medium flat silver tinsel
Wing: Yellow and red bucktail

Another traditional trout fly, the Mickey Finn, is a terrific crappie pattern. There used to be a rule of thumb for crappie fishin, "anything that has yellow in it will catch crappie." It may not be true, but the Mickey Finn has a lot of yellow in the wing and it catches crappie like crazy, so you can draw your own conclusions.

Fish it like other minnow-imitating patterns and try a faster-than-normal retrieve. We've had good luck by jerking the fly through the water 18 to 24 inches at a pop and then letting it sit for a few seconds before jerking it again. This technique works well when we're fishing parallel to ridges that drop off from shallow shorelines into 4 to 8 feet of water.

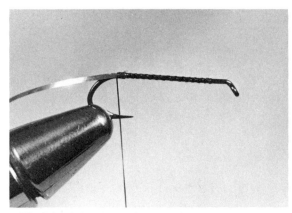

1. Place hook in vise and secure thread on hook shank above bend. Tie in a 6-inch length of flat silver tinsel at same point.

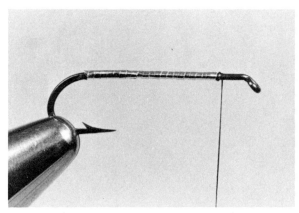

2. Wind thread forward to about 1/8 inch behind hook eye. Wrap tinsel forward to same point as thread forming body and tie off.

3. Tie in a small bunch of yellow bucktail at same point behind hook eye.

4. Tie a small bunch of red bucktail above yellow, and a second bunch of yellow over the red.

5. Trim the hair tips so none extend over hook eye, form head, whip finish, trim and cement.

BLACK-NOSED DACE BUCKTAIL

Materials:
Thread: Black, pre-waxed
Hook: Mustad 9672, sizes 6-12
Tag: Red floss
Body: Medium flat silver tinsel
Wing: Brown, black and white bucktail

This well-known trout pattern is excellent for taking crappie from very clear water. We like to fish the Black-nosed Dace deeper than other patterns and usually use it with a wet tip or sinking tip fly line. We retrieve it very slowly with 4 to 6-inch forward movements.

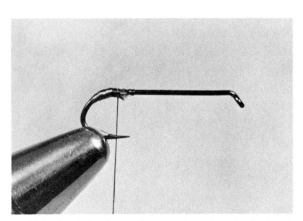

1. Place hook in vise and secure thread on hook shank at the bend. Tie in a short piece of red floss and wrap it 2 to 3 turns down bend forming tag. Tie off and cut.

2. Tie in a 4-inch piece of flat silver tinsel and wind thread forward to a point about 1/4 inch behind hook eye.

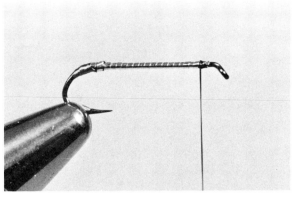

3. Wind tinsel forward keeping wraps close together but not overlapping. Tie off and trim excess tinsel.

4. Tie in a small bunch of white bucktail at point where tinsel was tied off.

5. Tie a small bunch of black bucktail above the white, and a small bunch of brown bucktail on top of the black.

6. Trim the butt ends of the bucktail fibers off so none extend over hook eye. Form head, whip finish, trim and cement.

145

MARABOU LEECH

Materials:
Thread: Black, pre-waxed
Hook: Mustad 9672, sizes 6-12
Body: Black, brown or olive dubbing
Upper body: Marabou to match body

Like the Woolly Bugger, the Marabou Leech pattern has excellent action in the water and catches several fish species. We've had our best luck fishing this pattern in areas of aquatic vegetation like cattails, lily pads and algae beds where leeches are normally found. It is usually most productive after Labor Day weekend and into the fall until the water turns cold and real leeches become dormant.

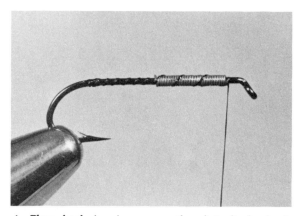

1. Place hook in vise, secure thread to hook shank above barb. Wrap lead wire from middle of hook shank to just behind hook eye. Wind thread forward over and through lead wraps. Cement to secure.

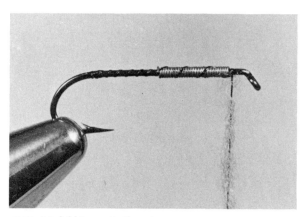

2. Twist dubbing onto thread.

3. Wrap dubbed thread back over hook shank toward bend forming body.

4. Tie in a bunch of marabou hackle fibers at bend of hook.

5. Dub thread lightly and continue adding small bunches of marabou fibers to top of fly body, working progressively closer to hook eye.

6. Tie in last bunch of marabou just behind hook eye. Form head, whip finish, trim and cement.

LEADWING COACHMAN WET FLY

Materials:
Thread: Black, pre-waxed
Hook: Mustad 3906, sizes 10-14
Tag: Flat gold tinsel or mylar
Body: Peacock herl
Hackle: Dark ginger hen - collar style
Wing: White duck wing quill segments

We use weighted and unweighted versions of the Leadwing Coachman Wet Fly mostly in the spring when the crappie are feeding heavily on nymphs because they are easy pickin's and are more readily available to the fish than some other forage. In moving water, like where a stream enters a lake, we free drift the fly, letting the current carry it along. When there isn't much current, we crawl the fly slowly across the bottom with an occasional short jerk, trying to imitate the nymph's natural movements.

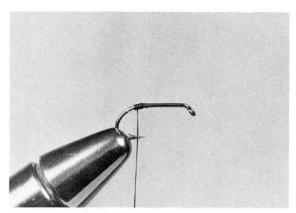

1. Tie on thread at bend of hook and attach gold tinsel at same point. Make two to three turns of tinsels to form tag. Tie off and trim.

2. Select three or four peacock herl and tie them on just in front of tag. Wind thread forward to a point slightly behind hook eye.

3. Wrap each herl forward separately to the point behind hook eye being careful not to mat fibers down. Tie off and trim.

4. Tie in a dark ginger hackle feather. Make two or three turns, tie off and trim.

5. Cut two small segments from matched white duck quills. Fit the segments together and with the wing tips pointing up, tie on top of hackle. Trim off butt ends that extend over hook eye.

6. Form head, whip finish and cement.

BLACK GHOST STREAMER (Bucktail wing)

Materials:
Thread: Black pre-waxed
Hook: Mustad 9672, sizes 6-12
Tail: Yellow hackle fibers
Body: Black floss
Rib: Flat silver tinsel
Throat: Yellow hackle fibers
Wing: White bucktail or white marabou

The Black Ghost Streamer is an excellent pattern for crappie, especially in the spring when they feed heavily on minnows. This pattern may be tied either weighted or unweighted to best meet the conditions where it is to be used. As with most other minnow imitations, try to retrieve the fly erratically, imitating the movements of an injured minnow. As a rule of thumb, use the bucktail version in stained water and the marabou-winged version in clear or flowing water where the extra seductive movement created by the marabou is beneficial.

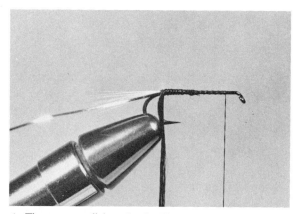

1. Tie on a small bunch of yellow hackle fibers for tail at point just above hook barb. At same point also tie on a 2-inch piece of flat silver tinsel, and on top of tinsel, tie on a 6-inch piece of black floss.

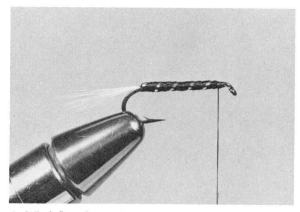

2. Wind floss forward to 1/8 inch behind eye of hook, then back to hook bend and then back toward eye again, forming a smooth body. Tie off floss and trim. Wrap tinsel forward in even wraps to rib the body. Tie off at same point as floss and trim.

3. To form throat, tie on a small bunch of yellow hackle fibers beneath the hook at same point as floss and tinsel were tied off.

4. Cut a small bunch of white bucktail to make the wing. Tie on at same point as other materials were tied off. The wing should extend back even with the tail. Trim butt ends of bucktail away from eye.

5. Form head, whip finish, trim thread and cement.

BLACK GHOST STREAMER (Marabou wing)

To tie this pattern, follow the above steps 1-3, then follow these steps:

1. Cut a small bunch of white marabou fibers from a plume and measure them to extend even with tail. Tie them on at point where other materials were tied off.

2. Form head, whip finish, trim thread and cement.

HELLGRAMMITE NYMPH
(The Poor Helgy)

Materials:
Thread: Black monocord
Hook: Mustad 9672, sizes 4-10
Tail: Dark moose body hair
Underbody: Lead wire
Body: Dark moose body hair
Wingcase: Black waterproof marker
Thorax: Tan chenille
Legs: Brown saddle hackle

The Hellgrammite Nymph is a very important pattern to the smallmouth bass fisherman. Smallmouths feed on these critters extensively and most probably pass up other forage in favor of a hellgrammite where they are found. If you are stream fishing for smallmouths, carry a variety of sizes and use them near rocks and deep-water pools.

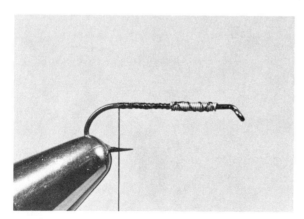

1. Beginning halfway down shank, wrap a piece of heavy lead wire forward to 1/4 inch behind hook eye. Wrap thread forward over lead wire then back to bend of hook to secure.

2. Cut a small bunch of dark moose hair, remove underfur and small hairs. Even tips in hair stacker. With thread directly above the barb, tie in moose hair with several tight wraps. Divide moose hair in half and make several wraps of thread around each bunch forming a forked tail.

152

3. Wrap thread forward over moose hair with several even wraps. Tie off moose hair as shown above. Trim butts.

4. Cover trimmed ends with thread forming smooth base for thorax. Select a saddle hackle and remove the fibers from one side of the feather and tie in where the body ends.

5. Tie in a piece of tan chenille where hackle feather was tied in.

6. Wrap chenille forward forming thorax, tie off and trim excess.

7. Wrap saddle hackle forward, ribbing thorax. Tie off and trim excess.

8. Form head, whip finish and cement. Trim hackle close along top of thorax. With black waterproof marker, mark the top of the chenille. Lacquer the moose hair body thoroughly.

CRAWDAD (pattern originated by Dave Whitlock)

Materials:
Thread: Pre-waxed (color to match body)
Hook: Mustad 9672, size 1
Antennae: Moose hair
Nose: Deer body hair (natural)
Pincers: Hen hackle feathers
Rib: Gold or copper wire
Eyes: Burned monofilament
Legs: Soft, webby grizzly hackle feather
Body: Translucent dubbing (choice of color)
Thorax: Same as body
Shell: Swiss straw, color to match body

Next to the hellgrammite nymph, crawdads (or crayfish) are the smallmouth's favorite forage. This crawdad pattern was developed by Dave Whitlock, and, like all of Whitlock's patterns, is very lifelike and effective. We use this pattern often when fishing rocky areas in reservoirs and lakes. It's a killer.

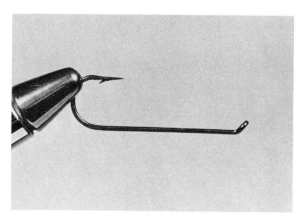

1. Put hook in vise upside down, with bend extending below the jaws of the vise.

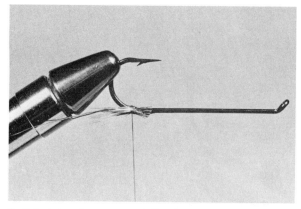

2. Select two long moose hairs for antennae. Tie them on at the bend on opposite sides of the hook so they curve away from each other. Cut a small bunch of deer hair and tie on between the moose hair antennae so that the natural tips extend a little way beyond the bend. DO NOT ALLOW DEER HAIR TO FLARE.

3. Select two soft, webby hen body hackles. Tie them on flat so they extend out from either side of the hook forming the fly's pincers.

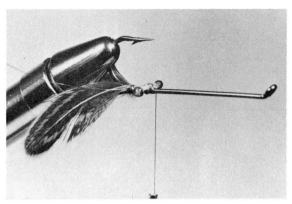

4. Tie on a 5- or 6-inch piece of copper or gold wire at the point where the pinchers were tied on. Bring thread forward to under hook point. Make monofilament eyes and tie them on under the hook point.

5. Tie a soft webby grizzly hackle feather on hook shank behind the eyes.

6. Wind thread back to bend of hook and spin dubbing onto thread. Wrap dubbed thread forward and figure-8 around the eyes. Continue wrapping forward to midway point on shank. Form a thick thorax by winding dubbed thread back and forth between eyes and middle of shank.

7. When thorax has been formed, rib it with grizzly hackle and tie off behind thorax. Trim excess hackle feather.

8. Wrap the front portion of the hook with narrow lead wire. Wind thread back and forth through the lead wire wraps to secure lead, leave thread behind thorax and cement the lead wraps liberally.

9. Cut a 3-inch piece of Swiss straw and place it along the lead wire on bottom of hook shank. Secure it by wrapping thread forward to the hook eye and back again. Leave excess straw extending out away from hook eye. Be sure to stop wrapping the thread at a point just behind the thorax.

10. Spin more dubbing onto the thread and wrap it toward the hook eye covering lead wire and Swiss straw. When finished, leave thread attached behind eye.

11. Cut two pieces of Swiss straw 3 to 4 inches long. Place one piece on top of the other and cut one end to a point. Place point against bend of hook and wrap over it with wire and make a wrap behind the monofilament eyes, lift up straw and make one wrap under the thorax, then lay straw down again and wrap wire forward forming rib over straw along body, ending rib ahead of hook eye where thread was left. Tie off wire and trim excess.

12. To form tail, separate the two pieces of Swiss straw that form the top of the crayfish so there is one piece on each side of the hook eye. Carefully pull the straw under the eye along with the first piece of straw and all three pieces form the fan tail of the crayfish. Trim these pieces as shown. Make several wraps of thread close to eye to finish fly. Use a permanent black marker to color eyes and the sides of Swiss straw on top of thorax. Also mark the edge of the fan tail.

WATER BEETLE

Materials:
Thread: Black pre-waxed
Hook: Mustad 3906, sizes 14-20
Shell: Gray goose wing segment
Hackle: Black hackle feather
Body: Peacock herl

Water Beetles are easy prey for the fish because the insects move relatively slow. Cast your imitation near vegetation or a rocky shoreline on a warm evening when the water is calm and skitter it slowly across the surface to attract smallmouths.

1. Cut a slip of grey fibers, about 1/4-inch wide, from a goose wing feather and tie it onto hook shank above the barb. At the same place tie in a black hackle feather and two peacock herl in that order. Be sure goose feather slip extends out behind hook bend.

2.Wind peacock herl forward to just behind hook eye forming body. Tie off and trim herl.

3. Wind hackle feather forward Palmer style to same point as herl. Tie off and cut.

4. Clip hackle fibers close to body on top and bottom of fly. Bring goose feather slip forward over the top of the body forming the body shell. Form head, whip finish and cement.

LEECH (pattern as tied by Thom Green)

Materials:
Thread: Pre-waxed to match body
  (black, brown, olive green)
Hook: Mustad 9672, sizes 2-10
Body: Mohair (black, brown, or olive green)
Tail: Marabou to match body
Hackle: Soft to match body

   Leeches glide, slide, and twist through the water in a series of movements that are irresistible to hungry smallmouth bass. Try fishing them slowly, giving the marabou tail a chance to pulsate and dance in the water. Keep a good grip on your rod and keep the line tight so you can react instantly when a bass latches onto your leech.

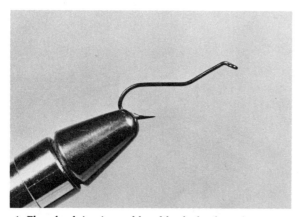

1. Place hook in vise and bend hook shank as shown.

2. Tie on a thick bunch of marabou on shank above hook barb for tail. Trim butt ends of fibers very close.

3. Wrap rear 1/3 of hook shank with lead wire.

4. Tie a 6-inch piece of mohair on to the hook shank at same point as marabou tail was tied.

5. Form tapered body by wrapping mohair heavily at the rear, tapering toward the hook eye.

6. Tie in a soft hackle feather behind the hook eye.

7. Make only one or two turns of hackle, keep it very sparse.

8. Form head, whip finish and cement. Cut tail straight – should be 2/3 the length of the body.

PHEASANT HOPPER

Materials:
Thread: Black pre-waxed
Hook: Mustad 9671, sizes 8-14
Tail: Dark moose hair
Body: Light brown fine chenille
Rib: Brown hackle
Wing: Mottled pheasant feather
Underwing: Deer hair
Collar: Deer hair
Head: Trimmed deer hair

The Pheasant Hopper is a high-floating grasshopper imitation that really makes smallmouths sit up and take notice in late summer and fall when there are grasshoppers everywhere. It is not difficult to tie and I enjoy fishing it because smallmouth usually hit hard in a spectacular strike. Cast it near vegetation and keep the hook sharp.

1. Tie in a small bunch of moose hair at bend of hook forming tail, tie in a 6-inch piece of chenille and a hackle feather (convex side toward the hook shank), in that order, at same spot moose hair is tied.

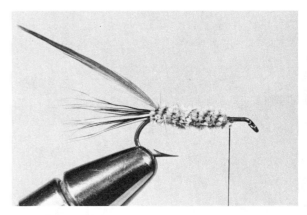

2. Before winding chenille forward, make one wrap behind the feather, and wrap chenille forward on hook shank to form body. Tie chenille off about 1/4-inch behind hook eye.

3. Wrap hackle feather forward, Palmer style, through body as shown, tie off and trim.

4. To form body, apply a small amount of dubbing to thread. Begin winding it around hook shank at bend and stop just behind tail.

5. Select a church window-type pheasant feather with good markings for overwing and remove webbing from stem.

6. Coat feather fibers lightly with cement and pull feather through your fingers to stick fibers together to give the overwing strength and narrow its width.

7. Tie feather on over deer hair underwing. Be sure feather lays flat, parallel to fly body.

8. Tie a small bunch of deer hair to side of the hook nearest you, and another on the opposite side. If deer hair doesn't cover hook shank to the eye, add another small bunch ahead of the others. Tie off with thread, whip finish and cement thread wraps. Trim head as shown.

FLOATING MAYFLY

Materials:
Thread: Color to match body
Hook: Mustad 94840, sizes 12-20
Tail: Dun hackle fibers
Body: Dubbing (olive, tan, brown,
  yellow or gray)
Wing-case: Dark dun poly dubbing
Legs: Dun hackle fibers

Smallmouth bass eagerly take mayflies when they are available. The Floating Mayfly is effective if you fish it with a great deal of patience and concentration. It must be fished on a floating line and long (7 1/2- to 12-foot) leader and it must be allowed to sit motionless on the water for extended periods of time — at least 2 or 3 minutes, which seems like a long time to me when I'm fishing. I've never had much luck skating the pattern across the surface, most of the action occurs when it's just sitting there. The majority of the strikes have happened just like a bluegill sucking a mosquito from the surface: the bass slowly floats up near the surface behind the fly, flares its gills, and inhales the fly. Nothing spectacular happens until you set the hook, then the fun begins. Keep your line tight and strike as soon as the smallmouth takes the fly and turns his body to sink back deeper in the water.

1. Tie on thread about 1/3 of the way behind hook eye. Apply dubbing to about 4 inches of the thread.

2. Slide dubbing down thread to top of hook shank and form into ball by wrapping thread ahead of and behind dubbing to form wing-case.

3. Select stiff fibers from saddle hackle feather and tie them on to hook shank directly above point.

4. To form body, apply a small amouth of dubbing to thread. Begin winding it around hook shank at bend and stop just behind tail.

5. Divide tail fibers equally and take one or two turns of dubbing between them to keep them separated.

6. Continue winding dubbed thread to wing-case forming tapered body. Wind bare thread in front of wingcase to secure body. Tie in a dun hackle feather, concave side towards hook shank, just ahead of wingcase.

7. Wind feather two or three turns, tie off and cut. Pull fibers back along the sides and bottom of fly body. Secure fiber butts with several wraps of thread.

8. Add dubbing to a short length of thread and form dubbed head. Whip finish and cement.

ZUG BUG

Materials:
Thread: Black pre-waxed
Hook: Mustad 3906B, sizes 10-16
Tail: Peacock sword fibers
Body: Peacock herl
Rib: Flat or oval gold tinsel
Wingcase: Mallard breast feather fibers
Beard: Brown hackle fibers

Though the Zug Bug is a pattern many fly rodders would choose for fishing brown and rainbow trout, few would use it when smallmouth bass fishing. But, guess what? It's a darn good smallmouth pattern for springtime fishing. One of the best places to fish it is at rocky creek inlets where cold, fresh water is pouring into the lake early in the year. Cast it upstream and let the current wash it into the lake past your position. Keep the rod tip high to control slack in the line, but let the fly bounce along the bottom in the current.

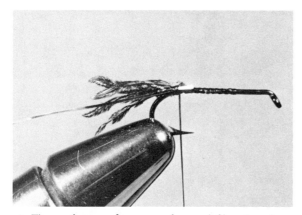

1. Tie on three or four peacock sword fiber tips above hook barb forming tail and tie 4-inch length of fine gold tinsel at same point.

2. Choose two or three heavy, full peacock herl and tie on above the tinsel.

3. Wrap thread forward to a point just behind the hook eye, then wrap peacock herl forward forming tapered body. Because the strands of peacock herl tend to separate as they are being wrapped, twist them together one-half turn with each wrap around hook shank. Tie off securely behind eye and trim.

4. Wind gold tinsel forward with even wraps ribbing the fly's body. Tie tinsel off and trim.

5. Coat mallard breast feather fibers with head cement, then cut a slip about 1/4 inch wide from one side of the feather. Tie on so it lays over the back of the fly (concave side down). Trim it so it is about one-half as long as the fly body.

6. Cut several fibers from a brown hackle feather and tie them on directly below fly body to form beard.

7. Form head, whip finish and cement.

BUMBLEPUP (Deer Hair Popper)

Materials:
Thread: Black pre-waxed
Hook: Mustad 9672, sizes 4-8
Tail: Black webby hackles
Body: Yellow dyed deer body hair

The Bumblepup deer hair pattern can turn an unproductive smallmouth fishing trip into an exciting evening in a matter of minutes. I'm not sure if the fish see the Bumblepup as a frog or a large insect, but I don't really care what they think it is because the important thing is they like it! Cast it near cover and let it sit awhile, then twitch it a bit and hang on. The powerful strike generally occurs when you first start to twitch the fly after a long pause. The Bumblepup is fun to tie and easy to fish. Carry a few in different sizes and colors.

1. Tie two black hackle feathers curving up and out (away from each other) onto the middle of the hook shank.

2. Cut a small amount of deer hair from skin patch and hold natural tips with your fingers. Spin deer hair by making a loop of tying thread around hair and hook shank and slowly tighten it, allowing hair to spin around hook. Make a half hitch with the thread and push hair back toward hook bend with fingers to make a compact deer hair body.

3. Cut another small bunch of deer hair, about one inch long, and trim natural tapered tips. Tie this bunch onto hook shank ahead of previous bunch and allow hair to flare around shank.

4. Keep adding small amounts of hair until there is just enough room behind hook eye to form a small head.

5. Tie a small amount of deer hair on top of the fly by parting the last section and laying a small amount of hair in the part. This hair will be kept entirely on top and is added to extend the hair over the eye of the hook.

6. Pull hair back with your fingers to make a small space to form head. Whip finish and cement.

7. Remove fly from vise to trim and shape body. Begin by turning fly over and trimming hair short on the bottom. Snip only a little hair away at a time. See photo for size and shape. Coat face of deer hair with cement to give it form and strength when it is popped in the water.

EXTENDED-BODY PARADRAKE

Materials:
Thread: Black pre-waxed
Hook: Mustad 94840, size 10
Body: Deer body hair
Hackle: Brown

When smallmouth bass are taking large flies from the surface, tie on an Extended-body Paradrake and get in on the action. Because it is a good-sized fly, the fish seem to think they have to hit it pretty hard. I've seen smallmouths miscalculate the fly's position and slap it 4 feet into the air missing the strike. I've had good luck with the fly in the evening when there is a slight chop on the water. Fish it near vegetatin adjacent to deep-water drop-offs for best success.

1. Cut a medium-sized bunch of deer hair, measuring it so it is about twice as long as the hook shank. Tie the base of the deer hair on about half-way down the hook shank.

2.Wrap thread behind the deer hair and half-hitch it so the hair extends toward the hook bend, but at an angle of about 45 degrees from the hook shank. Wrap butt ends of the clipped deer hair with thread so they are completely covered.

3. Form the extended body by ribbing the deer hair with even wraps of thread as it sweeps upward and back from the hook shank. When you come to the end of the body, make several wraps around the hair forming the tail, then wrap back toward the hook, crisscrossing the previous windings. When you reach the hook shank, wrap thread several times around hook and apply cement to entire deer hair body.

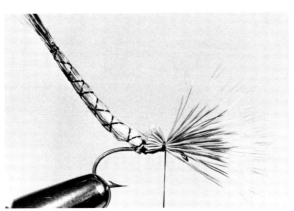

4. Tie on another small bunch of deer hair, this time allowing the natural hair tips to extend over the hook eye. Secure the hair butts with thread, Then trim them very short (portion nearest body).

5. Grasp the hair extending over the hook eye with your fingers and pull upright to form wing. Make several wraps of thread in front of the wing to hold it up. Next, wrap thread clockwise up the base of the wing a short distance and then wrap back down to shank. With thread behind the wing, wrap the butt ends of the deer hair (which are resting on the hook shank) down with the thread.

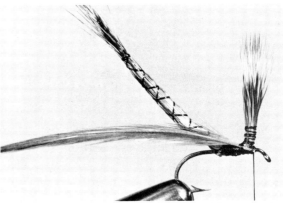

6. Tie two brown hackle feathers, shiny side up, to the base of the wing.

7. Wrap hackles horizontally around the wing's thread base. Tie feathers off and trim. Form head, whip finish and cement. Trim any hackle fibers that protrude below the hook.

MARABOU MINNOW

Materials:
Thread: Black pre-waxed
Hook: Mustad 9672, size 6
Body: Flat silver tinsel
Underwing: Marabou feather fibers
  (olive, yellow, orange, purple)
Sides: Mallard breast feathers
Throat: Marabou feather fibers (red)
Eye: Yellow and black lacquer

The Marabou Minnow is an excellent minnow imitation and is big and bulky enough for the fish to see easily. The large eye and the scale-like vermiculations of the mallard breast feathers add to its appeal. It is very effective when tied with a few wraps of lead wire around front portion of hook shank so it rises with each pull of the line, then dips, head-down, when there is a pause in the retrieve.

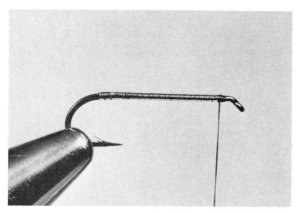

1. Tie 6-inch length of flat silver tinsel on at hook bend and wrap thread forward covering shank, then wrap tinsel forward over shank and thread forming body.

2. Trim a small bunch of yellow marabou feather fibers from plume, and tie on to top of hook shank about 3/16-inch behind hook eye. Fibers should sweep back over hook bend as shown. Trim butts as close as possible, then tie on succeeding small bunches of orange, purple and olive marabou fibers, each bunch on top of the last. This will create a full, whispy underwing/body for the fly.

170

3. Select two mallard body feathers of the same size with dark vermiculations. Tie one feather on each side of the hook (concave side toward the hook shank) and trim butts close to thread windings. Tie in a small bunch of red marabou feather fibers below the hook as a throat.

4. Wrap head, trim and cement. Marabou feather fibers should protrude from around body feathers.

5. Apply a small circle of yellow lacquer on each mallard breast feather as shown. When the yellow paint is dry, add a small circle of black lacquer within the yellow circle to create a large eye on each side of the fly.

BLACK & WHITE BUCKTAIL STREAMER

Materials;
Thread: Black monocord
Hook: Mustad 9672, sizes 2-8
Tail: Red hackle fibers
Body: Narrow flat silver tinsel
Throat: Long white hackle fibers,
  short red hackle fibers
Wing: Black & white kip tail

The Black and White Steamer is easy to tie and very effective when smallmouths are feeding on minnows. Start by fishing it deep with a sink-tip line, but if the action is slow or non-existent, try it at shallower depths with a floating line. We've found it is best to keep it as close to vegetation as possible and retrieve in an erratic manner.

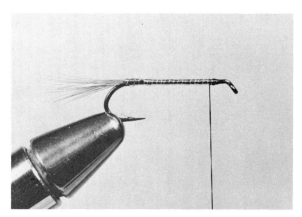

1. Tie red hackle fibers on shank above hook barb forming tail. Tie a 6-inch piece of tinsel on hook shank at the same point as tail is tied, then wrap tinsel forward along shank to a point about 1/8 inch behind hook eye forming fly body.

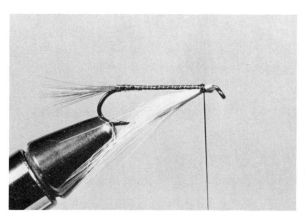

2. Form throat by tying on a small bunch of white hackle, a little longer than the length of the hook, below the hook shank and then tie in a small bunch of shorter red fibers, which are only half the length of the hook, at the same point.

3. To form wing, tie a small bunch of white kip tail on top of hook shank, then tie in an equal amount of black kip tail on top of the white.

4. Form head, whip finish and cement.

JOE'S HOPPER

Materials:
Thread: Black pre-waxed
Hook: Mustad 79671 or 9672, sizes 4-10
Body: Yellow chenille or wool
Wing: Two matched turkey quill sections
Tail: Red hackle fibers
Rib: Brown saddle hackle
Hackle: Brown and grizzly saddle
  hackle feathers

There are times in late summer and early fall when nothing catches largemouth bass like a grasshopper pattern and one of our favorites is Joe's Hopper. We tie this pattern in several different sizes and colors to imitate the different grasshoppers that are abundant throughout the Midwest. We try to make the hopper act like the real thing by casting and letting it sit on the water's surface for a few minutes before making it twitch by moving the rod tip. When a largemouth takes the hopper it usually takes it fast and hard, rather than slowly sipping it off of the surface like a dry fly. It's not unusual for the bass to jump completely out of the water and engulf the hopper on the way back down. Be sure to keep your fly line tight when fishing a hopper, or you will loose the bass when it strikes or makes its first run.

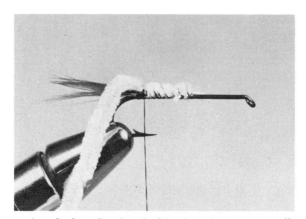

1. Attach thread at bend of hook and tie on a small bunch of red hackle fibers to form a tail.

2. Tie on a 6-inch length of yellow chenille in the middle of the hook shank and bind the chenille to the hook by wrapping with thread back to the spot the tail was tied.

3. Form a small loop of chenille at bend and tie vertically onto top of hook shank with thread.

4. Tie on a brown hackle feather at the same point as loop was tied. Wrap chenille forward to point about 1/4 inch behind hook eye forming body as shown. Tie off chenille and trim.

5. Wrap hackle forward around hook shank and through chenille, Palmer style, to front of body. Tie off and trim.

6. Trim hackle very short on each side of body. Cut two turkey quill sections about 1/8 inch wide and tie them on the sides of the fly one at a time.

7. Tie on one brown hackle and one grizzly hackle at the point where turkey sections were tied off. Wrap hackles forward individually to a point just behind hook eye. Secure with thread and trim.

8. Form a small head with thread, whip finish and cement. Trim turkey sections at an angle just behind chenille loop as shown.

KEEL HOOK STREAMER

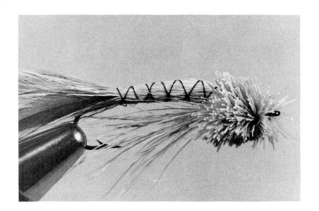

Materials:
Thread: Black pre-waxed
Hook: Mustad 79666, sizes 6-8
Tail: Yellow and brown hackle
Head: Yellow deer body hair

We use the Keel Hook Streamer for largemouth fishing when the fish are in dense cover that would be very difficult to fish with conventional flies. Because the keel hook rides up, the fly can be retrieved through and over weeds and other cover without getting snagged. If you are planning to do a lot of bass fishing, it will be worth your while to carry several of these flies in different sizes so you are prepared for any fishing situation.

1. Tie on thread in middle of hook shank and wrap forward to top of bend nearest the eye. Select two yellow hackles and two brown hackles. Match one yellow and one brown hackle feather and tie these on one side of the hook at top of bend, convex side toward the hook shank so they flare away from the shank. They should measure twice the length of the hook shank. Match the other feathers and tie on the same way on the other side of the hook.

2. Wrap thread forward to lower bend and tie on a small bunch of yellow deer hair. Spin deer hair in usual manner and lay the tips back along the hook shank.

176

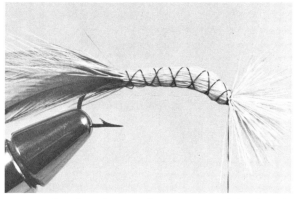

3. Wrap deer hair down with even wraps of the thread along hook shank. Advance thread to point in front of rear bend of hook, then wrap thread forward again with even wraps as shown, stopping behind ends of flared deer hair.

4. Tie on another small bunch of deer hair, keeping this bunch under the hook.

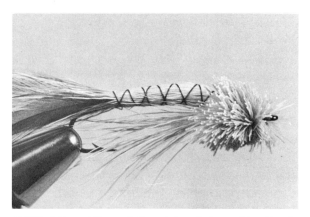

5. Wind thread through flared deer hair working it out onto bare hook. Add small bunches of deer hair until they reach hook eye. Make a few turns of thread in front of deer hair forming a small head, whip finish and cement.

6. Remove from vise and trim head as shown.

GRIZZLY KING STREAMER

Materials:
Thread: Black, pre-waxed
Hook: Mustad 9672, sizes 6-12
Tail: Red hackle fibers
Rib: Flat silver tinsel
Body: Green floss
Throat: Grizzly hackle fibers
Wing: Grizzly saddle hackles

The Grizzly King Streamer is an excellent minnow imitation for taking largemouth bass. It is especially productive when fished near submerged vegetation and along contours where shallow water drops off into deep channels — like submerged roadbed ditches or submerged creek channels. One of our favorite techniques is to weight the fly just behind the head and fish it on a sink-tip line. The sink-tip fly line helps keep the fly low in the water and lets you fish it near the bottom along the bases of submerged vegetation. Be sure to check the hook point often because fishing it near the bottom allows it to bump into rocks, sticks and other objects that may dull the point.

1. Tie on a small bunch of red hackle fibers at hook bend to form tail. Tie on a 2-inch piece of flat silver tinsel at the same point, followed by a 2-inch piece of green floss.

2. Wrap floss forward to form a smooth body. Tie off and trim floss just behind eye, leaving room for a small head.

3. Form rib by winding tinsel forward in even wraps. Tie off at same point as floss and trim. At that same point, tie grizzly hackle fibers to underside of hook shank to form throat.

4. Select four hackle feathers, all the same size. Place the curved sides of two hackle feathers together forming half of the wing. Do the same with the other two feathers. Place the second pair together with curved sides facing out to form complete wing. Tie wings onto hook, keeping them on top of hook shank and in a vertical position as shown.

5. Form head, whip finish and cement.

MUDDLER MINNOW

Materials:
Thread: Black, pre-waxed
Hook: Mustad 9672, sizes 1/0-12
Tail: Mottled turkey quill
Body: Flat silver tinsel
Underwing: Fox squirrel tail
Overwing: Mottled turkey quill
Collar: Deer body hair
Head: Deer body hair (clipped)

The Muddler Minnow is the best known and most productive of all trout fly patterns and it is fast becoming known as a largemouth bass killer, too. The muddler was originally tied to imitate a sculpin minnow, but through the years many variations of the original muddler have been developed and today different styles of the fly imitate other critters as well. The Muddler is effective for bass when fished on the surface, at mid-depths, and when bounced along the bottom. There are times when a fast surface retrieve brings bass boiling from hiding spots in shoreline vegetation, and there are times when it must be crawled very slowly across the bottom to entice a strike. We carry an assortment of Muddlers, both weighted and unweighted, in several sizes and colors.

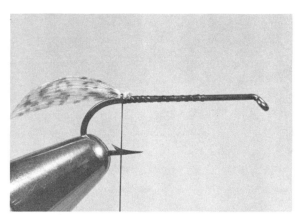

1. Cut turkey quill section about 1/8 inch wide and tie on at hook bend, making sure the natural tips point down. As you tie the turkey section on, push it forward slightly to give curve to the tail.

2. Tie on a 6-inch piece of silver tinsel at same point as tail. If fly is to be weighted, wrap lead 2/3 the way down the hook, wind thread through lead wraps and coat with cement to secure.

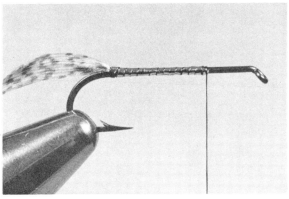

3. Wrap tinsel forward 2/3 of the way down hook shank as shown. Tie off and trim. Cover tinsel thoroughly with head cement.

4. Cut a small bunch of squirrel tail hair for underwing. Tie on at same point as tinsel was trimmed. Be sure underwing does not exceed the length of the turkey quill tial.

5. Cut another section of turkey quill and tie on above squirrel tail, pushing it forward as you tie it on to put a curve in the wing.

6. Make a smooth, even thread base on which to tie the deer hair. Wind thread to base of wing.

7. Cut a small bunch of deer hair and tie it on far side of the hook. Hair should flare but DO NOT ALLOW HAIR TO SPIN AROUND HOOK SHANK. Cut another bunch of hair and repeat the procedure, adding hair to the other side of hook.

8. Add small bunches of hair until they reach hook eye. Push hair back with thumb and forefinger to make a solid, compact bunch of hair. Make several turns of thread to secure hair, whip finish, trim thread and cement. Remove fly from vise and trim deer hair head as shown.

MARABOU MUDDLER

Materials:
Thread: Black, pre-waxed
Hook: Mustad 9672, sizes 2/0-12
Tail: Red hackle fibers
Body: Silver or gold tinsel
Wing: Marabou feathers in white,
  yellow, brown, black, olive
  (colors can be used singly or
  in combination), peacock herl
Head: Deer body hair (natural)

The Marabou Muddler was originally developed as a brown trout fly, but it is also dynamite for largemouth bass fishing. While it is sometimes weighted and fished near the bottom, this fly is most effective when fished as a top-water lure. The marabou feather wing gives the fly a soft, pulsating action as it floats on the water's surface. We like to cast this fly near heavy weeds, let it sit for a full minute or so and then pump the rod and retrieve the fly with long strips of the line. We tie it in a number of colors and sizes and have a good selection handy whenever we're after largemouth bass.

1. Tie on red hackle fibers at bend of hook for tail.

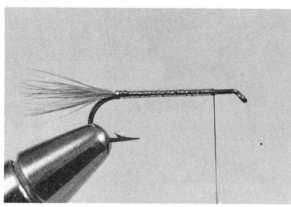

2. Tie on a 6-inch piece of flat silver or gold tinsel. If fly is to be weighted, wind lead wire 3/4 of the way down hook shank, then wind tinsel over lead to the same point. Tie off and trim.

3. Tie on marabou fibers for wing at spot tinsel was tied off.

4. Tie on four strands of peacock herl over marabou fiber wing.

5. Follow instructions for Muddler Minnow to form deer hair head.

6. Trim as shown.

SCULPIN MINNOW (Partridge Sculpin)

Materials:
Thread: Black, pre-waxed
Hook: Mustad 9672, sizes 2/0-6
Rib: Oval gold tinsel
Underbody: Lead wire
Body: Dark brown dubbing
Wing & Tail: Partridge (speckled)
  tail feathers
Fins: Hen pheasant shoulders, hen
  saddle tips, grouse shoulder
  or body feathers.
Head: Deer body hair dyed brown.

As is evident from the name, this is a Sculpin Minnow imitation, and we think it is a good one. There are two keys to this fly's success — its mottled coloration and its life-like movement in the water. We fish the sculpin close to, or right on, the bottom near submerged vegetation and along sharp drop-offs. This pattern is tied both weighted and unweighted, but because we like to fish it deep, we always use it with a sink-tip line.

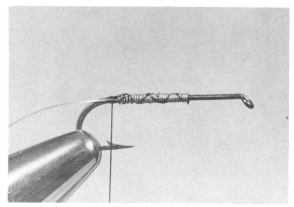

1. Wrap heavy lead on rear 2/3 of hook and cover with thread to secure. Tie on gold wire or gold braided oval tinsel at hook bend.

2. Dub thread and wrap forward forming a tapered body, tapering it gradually towards the front of the hook. Stop winding when body covers about 2/3 of the hook.

3. To make the wing, select two hen pheasant saddle hackles that have a large amount of web. Match them so their tips are even and strip the fibers from one side of both feathers for a distance about the same length as the body. Tie on with stripped quills fitting on top of the body.

4. Separate the feather barbules at rear of body, at the point where tinsel protrudes from body. Wrap tinsel through the feather securing it to top of body.

5. Wrap tinsel forward through feather and body creating rib. Tie off excess tinsel and trim.

6. Tie a smaller hen pheasant saddle hackle or breast feather on one side of the fly forming a pectoral fin. It should be 1/2 of the body length and should curve outward. Repeat process on the other side.

7. Cut a small bunch of deer hair and tie it on one side of the hook. Make several tight wraps of thread to flare the hair, but don't allow it to spin around the hook. Cut another bunch of deer hair and repeat process to other side. Add more deer hair building toward hook eye.

8. Remove fly from vise and trim as shown.

JIM'S CRAYFISH

Materials:
Thread: Brown or black, pre-waxed
Hook: Mustad 9672, sizes 2-6
Antennae: Two stripped brown
*   hackle stems*
Eyes: 30 lb monofilament melted
*   at both ends*
Pincers: Fox squirrel tail
Back: Fox squirrel tail
Underbody: Heavy lead wire
Body: Reddish-brown dubbing
Legs: Brown saddle hackle

Crawdads, also known as crayfish, are a favorite food of many predator species, most notably the smallmouth bass. But, largemouths are also fond of crawdads and will eagerly take them when they are available. When using a crawdad pattern, like Jim's Crayfish for largemouths, we fish them on the bottom near vegetation and rocks and use an alternating retrieve – allow the fly to sit a minute or so, then pull it 8 to 10 inches in quick spurts to imitate a live crawdad scurrying across the bottom. Then let the fly sit again. A largemouth usually attacks the fly when you jerk it across the bottom, so be ready and keep your line as tight as possible in anticipation of the strike.

1. Select two brown hackles and strip the fibers from 2 inches of the quills. Tie the hackle fibers in above the hook bend with curves facing out from each other (convex sides of the feathers toward the hook) creating antennae.

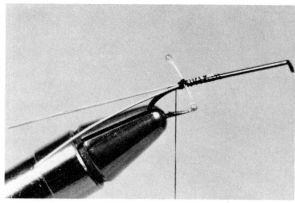

2. Cut a piece of monofilament and tie on at same point as antennae. It should be tied on across the hook with figure-8 wraps of thread. Trim so there is about 1/2 inch of monofilament extending on each side of the hook shank. Light a match and carefully touch it to each end of the monofilament to melt and form eyes.

186

3. Wrap thread about 1/2 way down hook shank and tie on a small bunch of fox squirrel tail. Wrap over the hair ends thoroughly and advance thread behind eyes.

4. Wind heavy lead wire from just behind the eyes to 1/3 of the way behind eye of hook as shown. Wrap thread back and forth through the lead securing it to the shank.

5. Tie on a small bunch of fox squirrel tail hair behind eyes on each side of hook. Be sure they extend a good distance past hook, because these bunches of hair will form the fly's pincers. Wrap thread around base of each pincer to bunch hair together.

6. Coat the tip end of each pincer with a small amount of head cement. Make an overhand knot around the end of each pincer with a short length of thread. Add another coat of head cement to the area. Trim ends as shown.

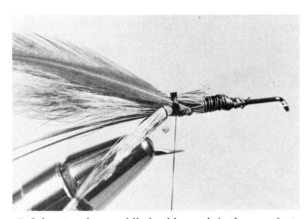

7. Select two long saddle hackles and tie them on just behind the eyes.

8. Apply dubbing to thread and wrap around pincer bases and beneath eyes.

9. Wind dubbing forward toward hook eye forming one layer of dubbing, then wind thread over the top of that first layer to secure it.

10. Apply more dubbing and lift pincers to wind dubbing beneath them. Continue wrapping dubbing toward hook eye, forming the body's second layer.

11. Wind hackles forward individually to a point 1/3 way down hook shank. Tie off and trim.

12. Trim hackle fibers short along the top of the fly.

13. Pull the bunch of squirrel tail hair between the pincers back over the top of the hook to form the back of the fly. At point where hackles were tied off, wrap thread over hair with several tight, evenly spaced turns just behind hook eye.

14. Wind several turns of thread just behind hook eye, whip finish and cement.